The North Country Guide to

Mountain Biking

Minnesota · Wisconsin

written by
CINDY STORM, CINDY BIJOLD, KELLEY OWEN,
ANNE BRECKENRIDGE

The North Country Guide To
Mountain Biking

"A trail guide to some of the best fat-tire riding in the upper midwest."

Copyright 1994 by White Pines Press
Revised 1998

Published by:
White Pines Press
5311 South Park Circle, Suite 300
Savage, MN 55378

Printed by:
Nystrom Publishing Co.
9100 Cottonwood Lane
Maple Grove, MN 55369

Printed in the United States of America

Cover Design: Kelley Graham
Book Layout: Anna Dvorak
Maps: Anna Dvorak and Mike Laudenslager
Cartoons: Shawn Van Briesen
Editors: Ken Storm Jr., Nancy Storm, Cindy Thompson and Neil Winston
Authors: Cindy Bijold, Cindy Storm, Kelley Owen, and Anne Breckenridge

ISBN 0-9640520-1-6

Acknowledgments

Writing a book can be like making a film. The public never sees all the sweat and hard work that it took to complete.

At our "Oscar" night our acceptance speech goes like this: We could not have accomplished our goal of publishing this book without the help and support of some very special people. We would like to thank:

Anna Dvorak: The map maker and author's caricatures. I cannot believe you are still speaking to us.

Mike Laudenslager: The other map maker. You even laughed when we brought you the 5 foot topo map.

Shawn Van Briesen: Our cartoonist was the only person to meet our original deadline. Was that sometime in 1993?

Ken Storm, Jr. and Nancy Storm: We know, we know, we are not Thoreau! Our famous editors.

Cindy Thompson and Neil Winston: The caped crusaders with their editorial "Bat Line."

Deb Juberian and Mason Owen: Our novice riding partners got the fat-tire fever and have not been off their bikes since.

Jim and Kris January: Jim says to Kris. . . "Honey I am going to research a ride with Cindy B. I PROMISE I will be back in an hour." Jim rode many of the rides with us and Kris supplied an enormous amount of support and tolerance.

Gary Crandall and Tom Schuler: A special thanks for your support of our book.

A special thanks to: MN DNR, WI DNR, WI Travel Bureau and US Forest Service.

A big THANK YOU to everyone. We had no clue the amount of work that is required to publish a book. This has truly been a learning experience for all four of us.

Sincerely,

Cindy Bijold, Anne Breckenridge, Cindy Storm and Kelley Owen

Introduction

Mountain biking is more than simply bicycling: It's transforming. A mountain bike helps you realize a new sense of freedom and adventure. As a needy escape of the cars, cell phones, and computers that clutter our lives, mountain biking shows you Mother Nature at her best.

Imagine it. Hearing an owl's call while mountain biking at night with lights. Sighting elk tracks. Taking in the scent of autumn's crisp leaves. Viewing Lake Superior from atop her majestic shoreline.

Hopefully through sharing our favorite trails, this new edition of the North Country Guide to Mountain Biking will open this world to you.

Happy Trails,
Cindy Bijold

Table of Contents

Forward

How to use this guide book 8

Riding Technique Tips 10

Mountain Bike Trail Tips 12

Section 1 ....NORTHERN MINNESOTA

Big Aspen Trail 20

Cascade Lodge 22

Gegoka / Flathorn..26

Gooseberry Falls State Park 28

Hidden Valley / Tezona Trail 30

Lake Bemidji State Park 32

Laurentian Trail - Giants Ridge 34

Lee Mines Trail 36

Lutsen Mountain Bike Park 38

McCarthy Beach State Park..40

Movil Maze 44

Pincushion Mountain..46

Scenic State Park 48

Silver Trail - Giants Ridge 52

Split Rock State Park 54

Whitefish Lake 58

Wynne Lake Overlook - Giants Ridge 60

Section 2 ....CENTRAL MINNESOTA

Continental Divide Trail...64

Cut Lake Trail...66

French Rapids Trail 68

Jay Cooke State Park 70

Paul Bunyan State Forest...72

Pillsbury State Forest 74

Savanna Portage State Park 76

Simpson Creek 78

Spider Lake Trail 80

St. Croix State Forest 82

St. Croix State Park 84

Sugar Hills Trail..86

Suomi Hill Trail 90

Washburn Lake Trail 94

Section 3 ....METRO / SOUTHERN MINNESOTA

Afton Alps 98

Battle Creek..100

Brightsdale Unit - R. Dorer State Forest 102

Bronk Unit - R. Dorer State Forest 104
Elm Creek Park Reserve 106
Kruger Unit - R. Dorer State Forest 108
Lake Elmo Park Reserve 110
Lawrence Unit - MN River Valley State Park 112
Lebanon Hills 114
Louisville Swamp - MN River Valley State Park 116
MN River Bottoms - Mounds Springs 118
Mount Kato Mountain Bike Park 120
Murphy-Hanrehan Park Reserve 122
Myre - Big Island State Park 124
Oakridge / Wet Bark Trail - R. Dorer State Forest 126
Reno Unit 128
Snake Creek Trail - R. Dorer State Forest 130
Trout Valley Trail - R. Dorer State Forest 132

Section 4 ....NORTHERN WISCONSIN

After Hours Ski Trail 136
Bar Stool Loop - CAMBA 138
Copper Falls State Park..140
Drummond Loop - CAMBA 142
Fire Tower Loop - CAMBA 144
Flambeau River State Forest..146
Oxbo Ski Trail 148
Patsy Lake Loop - CAMBA 150
Razorback Ridges 152
Rock Lake - CAMBA 154
Sleigh Trail - CAMBA 156
Tall Pines Loop - CAMBA 158
The North Country Trail 160
Valkyrie North Trail 162

Section 5 ....SOUTHERN WISCONSIN

Governor Dodge State Park 166
Lake Wissota State Park 168
Kettle Morain - Emma Carlin 170
Kettle Morain - John Muir 172
Kettle Morain - Northern Unit 174
Mirror Lake State Park 176
Perrot State Park 178
Smrekar Trail - Black River State Forest 180
Wildcat Trail - Black River State Forest 182

Minnesota & Wisconsin State Bike Trails 188
About the Authors 194

How to Use This Guide Book

Ride Time
Ride time is based on the average rider. Allow extra time to birdwatch, relax or picnic.

Terrain
Each ride will describe the type of the trail and its surface.

Distance
Round trip mileage is usually indicated. Mileage was calculated using a bicycle cyclometer. Be aware that bicycle computers vary, and slight differences in mileage may occur.

Rating
Trails vary greatly as does the fitness level and riding skill of each mountain biker. Ratings provide only a general idea of trail difficulty.

CHOOSE A RIDE WITHIN YOUR ABILITY

Easy Trail
Lower levels of physical exertion required. Climbs and descents are gentle. There are few technical obstacles on the route. The trail surface is firm and not usually wet. Length of route is short.

Moderate Trail
Physical exertion is moderate. Technical skills should allow you to maneuver over small obstacles on the trail. Climbs and descents are more demanding. Portaging your bike may be necessary. Ride length is somewhat longer. Trail surface may be soft.

Advanced Trail
High levels of physical exertion. Good riding skills are required to negotiate the route. Long, steep climbs and technical descents are common. Portaging your bike may be necessary. Ride distance and time maybe long. Trail surface may be soft, wet, sandy or loose soil.

Maps

Every attempt has been made to provide an accurate trail map. However, conditions do change, especially in active logging areas. We strongly recommend checking with local bike shops, State Parks, the DNR or the US Forest Service to determine conditions of a particular trail.

Access

Directions are provided to the trailhead from the nearest city. Each ride will have an overview map with a marker to locate what part of the state the ride is located. Please park well off any roadway and have respect for all private property.

Ride Overview

Background information provides you with interesting tidbits of historical, geological or wildlife information. We have also included where drinking water and restrooms can be found.

RIDE WITH THE ENVIRONMENT IN MIND!

Trail Directions

Detailed route descriptions are provided for each ride. Mileage markers are given to help orient you along the route. Before attempting a route, read the trail directions to determine the type of ride you desire. Included in the description will be points of interest. Check your mileage at specific intersections for quick reference to the map.

Remember, changes can and do occur. If you encounter changes or errors please let us know. Our address is provided at the back of the book. Telephone numbers for the governing agency of each ride are listed. We suggest calling to obtain additional, detailed maps of the surrounding areas. Please call ahead to determine the current status and condition of the route you wish to ride. Some routes may be closed due to excessive wetness or changes in land access.

ALWAYS RIDE SAFELY!

You are responsible for your own safety. Do not attempt trails that are beyond your skill level. **Always wear a helmet.** Ride in pairs, control your speed and let someone know where you are going. Most state forests are not equipped for on trail rescue so make sure that whatever you get yourself into you can get yourself out of.

Riding Technique Tips

Climbing:

Individual preference determines whether to sit or stand while climbing. Whatever your choice, body position on the bike is crucial to a successful climb. If you stay seated, inch yourself to the front edge of the saddle. This will keep your front wheel in contact with the ground, but still provide enough weight over the rear wheel for traction. For those who wish to stand, keep your weight over the crank arms to insure that your back wheel has adequate weight and does not spin out. With the advent of front suspension and the inherent flex that accompanies them, the seated position is more efficient.

Descending:

Always control your speed. Stand up and move your weight back. This can be accomplished by placing your rear end behind the saddle which will keep you from going over the handlebars. Let your elbows and knees act as shock absorbers. Control your speed before encountering the descent.

Shifting:

Many mountain bikers have walked their bikes out of the woods due to a broken chain from improper shifting. The key is to anticipate the climb and shift to a lower gear before resistance is placed on the chain. You can also down shift in the middle of a climb by letting up briefly on the pedals as you shift to a lower gear. Even with the advent of the new "hyperglide" systems you can save stress and wear on your chain by following the above advice.

Braking:

One of the greatest causes of trail damage is caused by improper braking. This leads to erosion and washouts of corners. The best thing a mountain biker can do to minimize the impact is to control ones speed and apply equal amounts of pressure to both the front and rear brake. NEVER SKID! The front brake provides far more stopping power than the rear. Bike mechanics can spot a rookie by seeing that the rear brake pads are worn while the front pads look brand new. Apply power to both front and rear brakes and you will never be launched over the handlebars. You will be amazed at the control provided. This will help keep a trail open and keep trail maintenance to a minimum.

Obstacles:

Stand up. Relax your hands, arms, and most importantly, your knees. Grip the saddle with the inside of your thighs to provide stability and lateral control. Your weight should be shifted slightly to the rear to allow you to lift the front wheel over obstacles. As you go over the object, allow your knees to flex and absorb the impact of your rear wheel riding over the obstacle. Another tip: Keep your pedals parallel to the ground for the best clearance.

For Experts Only:

Bunny hop your bike: Have your feet strapped or clipped firmly to your pedals. Squat down and vault your body straight up. This lifts your bike, front and rear, equally off the ground. With enough speed your momentum will carry you over the obstacle.

Mountain Bike Trail Tips

Rules Of The Trail:

Mountain biking is a relatively new sport, therefore we as mountain bikers are utilizing trails established by hikers, horseback riders and snowmobilers. Multi-use conflicts and land access issues can be minimized by riding responsibly. If we follow simple but important trail etiquette we can promote mountain biking as a positive sport.

- **Yield right of way to hikers.**
  Avoid surprising hikers. Call out a basic "hello" and ask to pass.

- **Yield to horses.**
  Horses spook easily. Stop, get off your bike and allow horseback riders to pass you.

- **Ride only on trails that are open to mountain biking.**
  Respect trail closures and private property.

- **Ride with the environment in mind.**
  Control your speed, *never skid!* Do not ride if the trail is excessively wet. Pack out what you pack in. Stay on the trail.

- **Be prepared.**
  Know yourself, your equipment and the area you intend to ride.
  Always carry plenty of water, spare tubes and tools.
  Carry clothing for inclement weather.

- **Get involved.**
  Volunteer for organizations providing trail maintenance or new trail access. Offer your assistance to land managers in whatever capacity they may require (trail maintenance or possibly trail patrol).

Back-Country Check-List

Anytime you ride off road be self-sufficient. Make sure your bike is in good working condition. Be prepared to make minor bike repairs. Bring food and plenty of liquids.   Carry the essentials you need to handle most any situation. Another tip: Tuck a few dollars into your tool kit for emergencies.

Tools/Miscellaneous:

- High Energy Foods
- Spare Tube
- Tire Irons
- Chain Tool
- Tool Mate*
    - *4,5,6mm Allen Wrenches
    - *Flat Head Screwdriver
    - *Phillips Screwdriver
    - *6" Crescent Wrench
- Pack Jacket

- Rack Strap
- Patch Kit
- Frame Pump/CO2 Cartridges
- Spoke Wrench
- Compass
- Map
- Pocket Knife
- Water
- Duct Tape for tire rips
- First Aid kit

What To Wear:

A pair of comfortable bike shorts and a biking jersey with pockets is a good combination and always wear a helmet. As the weather cools in the fall the layer system works best. If riding during the hunting season wear florescent orange clothing, and make your presence known well in advance. **We DO NOT recommend riding during the hunting season.**

Choose Your Ride:

Choose your ride with your ability and physical condition in mind. Mountain biking can be a strenuous sport. Many trails provide resistance even if they are flat. Most rides are well suited to the average rider, but keep in mind that riding 5 miles off road is similar to riding 10 miles on road.

RIDES BY NUMBER

Section 1 NORTHERN MINNESOTA

1   Big Aspen Trail
2   Cascade Lodge
3   Gegoka / Flathorn
4   Gooseberry Falls State Park
5   Hidden Valley / Tezona Trail
6   Lake Bemidji State Park
7   Laurentian Trail - Giants Ridge
8   Lee Mines Trail
9   Lutsen Mountain Bike Park
10   McCarthy Beach State Park
11   Movil Maze
12   Pincushion Mountain
13   Scenic State Park
14   Silver Trail - Giants Ridge
15   Split Rock State Park
16   Whitefish Lake
17   Wynne Lake Overlook -
    Giants Ridge

Section 2 CENTRAL MINNESOTA

18   Continental Divide Trail
19   Cut Lake Trail
20   French Rapids Trail
21   Jay Cooke State Park
22   Paul Bunyan State Forest
23   Pillsbury State Forest
24   Savanna Portage State Park
25   Simpson Creek
26   Spider Lake Trail
27   St. Croix State Forest
28   St. Croix State Park
29   Sugar Hills Trail
30   Suomi Hill Trail
31   Washburn Lake Trail

Section 3 METRO / SOUTHERN MINNESOTA

32   Afton Alps
33   Battle Creek
34   Brightsdale Unit -
    R. Dorer State Forest
35   Bronk Unit -
    R. Dorer State Forest
36   Elm Creek Park Reserve
37   Kruger Unit -
    R. Dorer State Forest
38   Lake Elmo Park Reserve
39   Lawrence Unit -
    MN River Valley State Park
40   Lebanon Hills
41   Louisville Swamp -
    MN River Valley State Park
42   Mounds Springs -
    MN River Bottoms
43   Mount Kato Mountain Bike Park
44   Murphy-Hanrehan Park Reserve
45   Myre - Big Island State Park
46   Oakridge/Wet Bark Trail -
    R. Dorer State Forest
47   Reno Unit
48   Snake Creek Trail -
    R. Dorer State Forest
49   Trout Valley Trail -
    R. Dorer State Forest

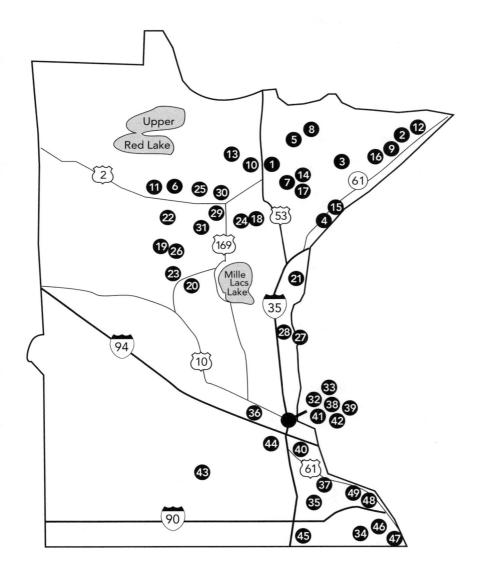

RIDES BY NUMBER

Section 4   NORTHERN WISCONSIN

49 Trout Valley Trail -
50 After Hours Ski Trail
51 Bar Stool Loop - CAMBA
52 Copper Falls State Park
53 Drummond Loop - CAMBA
54 Fire Tower Loop - CAMBA
55 Flambeau River State Forest
56 Oxbo Ski Trail
57 Patsy Lake Loop - CAMBA
58 Razorback Ridges
59 Rock Lake - CAMBA
60 Sleigh Trail - CAMBA
61 Tall Pines Loop - CAMBA
62 The North Country Trail
63 Valkyrie North Trail

Section 5   SOUTHERN WISCONSIN

64 Governor Dodge State Park
65 Lake Wissota State Park
66 Kettle Morain - Emma Carlin
67 Kettle Morain - John Muir
68 Kettle Morain - Northern Unit
69 Mirror Lake State Park
70 Perrot State Park
71 Smrekar Trail - Black River State Forest
72 Wildcat Trail - Black River State Forest

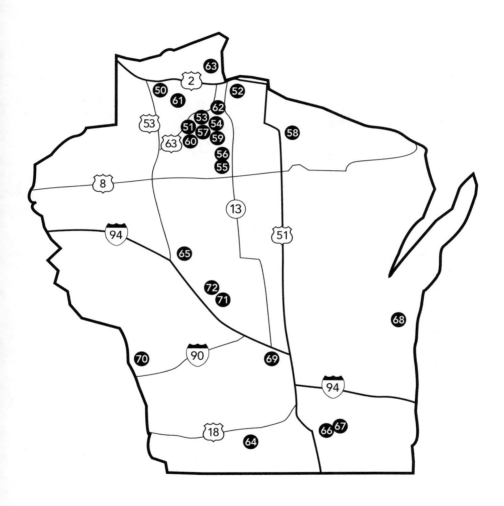

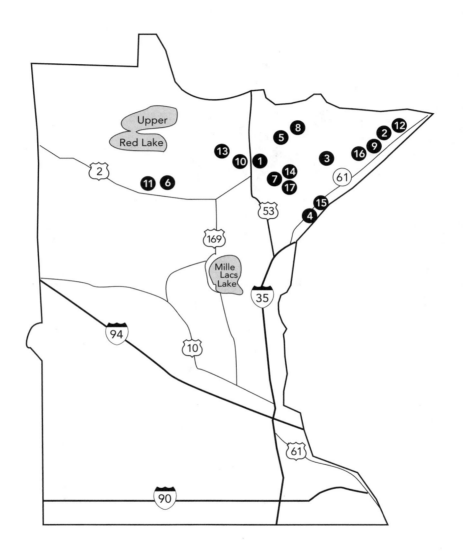

The North Country Guide to
Mountain Biking

SECTION 1

Northern Minnesota

1   Big Aspen Trail

2   Cascade Lodge

3   Gegoka / Flathorn

4   Gooseberry Falls State Park

5   Hidden Valley / Tezona Trail

6   Lake Bemidji State Park

7   Laurentian Trail - Giants Ridge

8   Lee Mines Trail

9   Lutsen Mountain Bike Park

10   McCarthy Beach State Park

11   Movil Maze

12   Pincushion Mountain

13   Scenic State Park

14   Silver Trail - Giants Ridge

15   Split Rock State Park

16   Whitefish Lake

17   Wynne Lake Overlook - Giants Ridge

Big Aspen Trail
Virginia, MN   (218) 229-3371

Distance: 8.5 miles
Ride time: 1.5-2 hours

Trail: Rolling, hard-packed ski trails
Rating: Moderate to Advanced

Access: Big Aspen is 11 miles north of Virginia, MN. Take Highway 53 north for 8 miles. Turn northeast on 131 for 1 mile. Turn west on County Road 68 for .3 miles. Straight on County Road 405 for 2 miles.

Hidden deep in the Superior National Forest, Big Aspen boasts 20 miles of trails from easy to challenging. The trails pass through mature stands of pine and hardwood forest plus new-growth forest. Several scenic vistas make this trail especially popular in the fall.

0.0 mi.   Park at the trailhead. The trail starts across the road, diagonally to the left, from the parking lot. The trail won't be mowed but enough locals use the trail that it is ridable. Pedal 1 mile to the first junction (8). The ride will be bumpy, but it does get better.

1.0 mi.   Turn right at jct. 8. Cruise nearly .5 miles downhill on a smooth trail. At the bottom of the hill veer left for the suggested route (7). The trail is wider and less rocky. Pedal through stands of young white pines and grassy meadows.

2.6 mi.   The trail splits at jct. 13. Go left and pedal .6 miles under a canopy of aspens. At jct. 12 you may want to take a left and pedal up to the shelter. You will find a stunning view of Superior National Forest.

3.2 mi.   The trail "Y's" at jct. 14. The route to the right becomes very wet and boggy. Take a left and climb a rocky incline for .3 miles. Sections of the forest have been heavily logged, but are now regenerating with young stands of aspens and red and white pines.

3.6 mi.   At the top of the incline (15), take the trail to the right on the outside loop. Traverse the ridge on an easy grade. Your reward will be a beautiful overview of the forest. In the fall, pockets of red maples and rich evergreens interweave with the golden aspens.

3.8 mi.   Tear yourself away from the view and head down into the valley. The trail smooths out as it squirts you through a short corridor of sugar maples.

4.2 mi.   At junction 25 there is a grove of mature aspens. Turn right for the outside loop. The trail will be a little rocky as you ride above the lake to your left. Be careful coming off the ridge; there is a rocky drainage near the bottom. A log shelter near the tamarack bog makes a great fall picnic spot.

4.5 mi.   At jct. 26 stay to the right for the suggested ride. Beware there is a technical climb.

5.0 mi.   At jct. 28 turn right and cross FR 257. Pedal through open meadows along the edge of the forest. This trail is less traveled and not marked.

6.4 mi.   The trail comes out onto FR 257. Pedal south 2 miles back to the trailhead for a total of 8.5 miles.

Big Aspen Trail

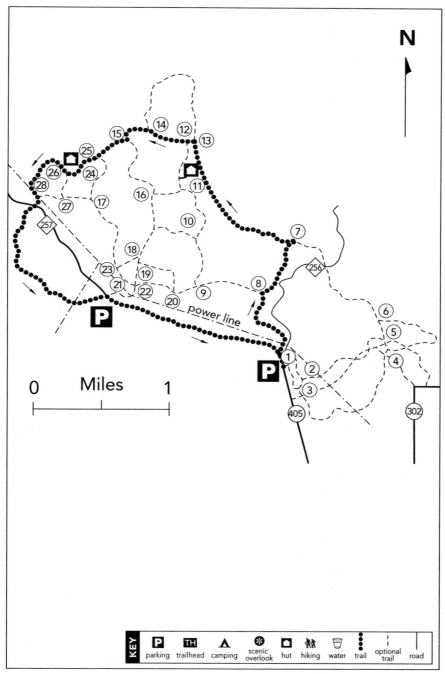

Maps are reproduced from USDA Forest Service Paul Witte, Cartographer (414) 297-3403.

21

Cascade Lodge
Tofte, MN   (218) 387-1112

Distance: 13 miles   **Trail:** Ski trails and old logging roads
Ride time: 2.5 hours   **Rating:** Moderate

Access: Cascade Lodge is 90 minutes north of Duluth on Hwy 61. All amenities are available including cabins and a restaurant.

The Cascade Lodge is nestled along the Cascade river with its rushing waterfalls and wonderful biking and mountain biking trails. The Cascade trail climbs to one of the highest elevations in Minnesota at 1880 feet.

0.0 mi.   Pedal up the service road past the log cabins and hop on the trails just beyond the maintenance garage. Follow the sign to the left towards "Lookout Mountain". Pass the "Wildflower Trail" (hiking trail) and roll along the edge of the woods.

0.1 mi.   Duck into the woods to your right and gradual climb under a canopy of birch and aspen. Head to the right towards the "Pioneer Trail" and continue to gradually climb.

0.4 mi.   Pedal through the clearing and cross over the Superior Hiking Trail. At the Pioneer loop, stay right and pedal through aspen stands along the Cascade Creek.

2.4 mi.   Where the trail "T"'s turn right towards "Deer Yard Lake"

2.5 mi.   Follow the old forest road to the right. The ski trail straight ahead is impassable in the summer due to a busy beaver. The old road passes by marshes and rolls up to give you fantastic glimpses of the Superior National Forest.

3.6 mi.   The dirt trail ends at a large intersection. Take the gravel road to the left (look for red and white bike marker). This is a nice change of pace; you can actually look around as you ride on this perfectly graded gravel road.

4.2 mi.   Look for the ski trails to start on the left near a stand of white pine saplings. There may be an old marker here. (DON'T FOLLOW THE BIKE MARKER UP THE ROAD.)

4.4 mi.   Take the right hand route. Pass by a gate. The trail is fairly flat, but a little rocky making it a little more technical to navigate.

5.3 mi.   Cross a small creek and pedal a short distance to Deer Yard Lake. Past the lake the trail is rugged, wet, rocky and rough, but hang tough it's only for one mile.

7.1 mi.   Follow the ski trail as it bends to the left. An old forest road continues straight ahead. Look for a natural spring in this area.

8.4 mi.   Pass a short loop trail on the right. Ride ahead 50 feet and look for the trail that climbs up to 1880 ft. to the old Cascade Fire Tower site. The tower is long

Continued on page 24

Cascade Lodge

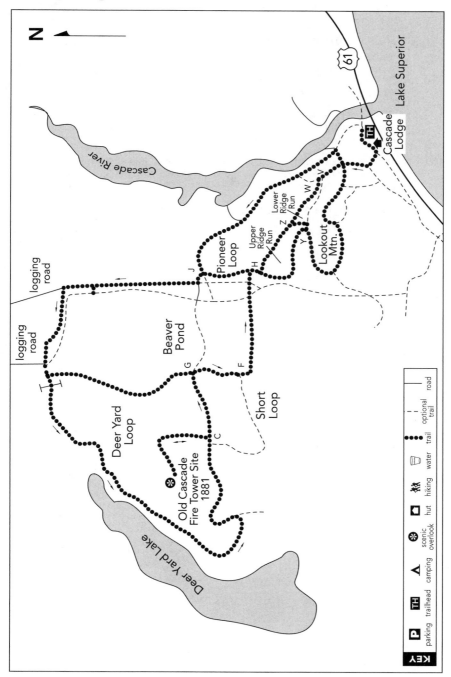

KEY

P parking	**TH** trailhead	**▲** camping	**⊛** scenic overlook	**☐** hut	**☌** water	**森** hiking

•••• trail

- - - optional trail

——— road

gone, but it is a great ride. Over 1 mile of climbing means a great ride back down the hill!

9.5 mi.   At intersection "G" take the trail to the right (FR 333). This trail is less traveled but has good roll.

10.0 mi. The ski trail (blue diamond marker) takes a sharp right, but continue on the trail straight ahead.

10.3 mi. The old two-track goes through an open area and rolls down to a creek crossing. This is an old homestead. You will see the remnants of its inhabitants. Look for the trail to continue to the right of the clearing.

10.8 mi. The two track dog-legs left. Take a small overgrown trail straight ahead. You may have to bushwhack a short distance but this puts you back on the ski trails.

12.3 mi. Cruise through jct. V and coast downhill all the way back to the parking area!

12.8 mi. Don't go so fast you forget to turn left!

Do you think the boys at Rock Shox
would be interested in this new design?

Gegoka - Flathorn
Isabella, MN   (218) 323-7676

Distance: 25 miles
Ride time: 3-5 hours

Trail: Remote, old forest roads
Rating: Easy to Moderate

Access: From the North Shore take Highway 61 to Highway 1. Six miles west of Isabella, MN.

The Gegoka - Flathorn trail system is in the Superior National Forest. Dotted with numerous ponds, lakes and wetlands, the trail winds through a diverse range of terrain and landscape. Parts of the trail system were designed for skiing and can be wet during the summer. The suggested ride avoids these areas.

0.0 mi.   Pedal west on Highway 1 for .5 miles and turn right. The backside of a stop sign is the only indicator that you have the right road. Cruise on the flat, two-track for 1.1 miles. Notice several uncut spurs and a small lake to the left. The trail will become more rolling.

2.0 mi.   Stay to the right at jct. 11, and bear right through the next two intersections. At jct. 10 turn left for the long loop. Several trails are uncut due to wet areas.

3.5 mi.   The road will "T" at a more developed road. Turn left and pedal on FR 177 for 2.3 miles. Notice several small lakes on either side of the road.

5.8 mi.   Pass Grouse Lake Road. Here the road narrows and becomes more rugged. There will be several spurs on both sides of the road. Most of these are short accesses to the lakes that flank the forest road. Where the road splits stay to the left.

6.6 mi.   This rolling forest road is canopied with the foliage of a mixed hardwood forest. Several rocky downhills will require concentration. For the most part it is an enjoyable, leisurely ride.

7.9 mi.   At the "Y" in the road, turn left and follow the road through pine forest and along wetlands. This is a perfect area for spotting wildlife.

9.4 mi.   The double-track ends on a well traveled gravel road. Turn left onto FR 377 and pedal for 2.2 miles.

11.6 mi.   Turn left onto FR 386. You will be back onto a narrow two-track. You will notice several trails on both sides of the road. These trails are used for hunting or to access small lakes. On the main trail pedal through pine forests that turn into beautiful stands of birch and aspen.

14.1 mi.   At the "Y" in the road stay to the right. You will see Surprise Lake to the left. A small footpath takes you down to the lake for a swim or picnic. This is a slice of heaven in the fall when the maples add a sprinkling of color to the beauty of the lake.

15.2 mi.   Pedal on a two-track along a bog. At the stop sign turn left on to FR 383. Pedal .5 miles. Pass Grass Lake on your left. You may not see the lake because of the lush undergrowth.

17.2 mi.   The trail will "Y". Stay on the main forest road to the right for 3.5 miles. The
           forest road ends at Highway 1. Turn east (left) and pedal 3.5 miles back to the
           National Forest Lodge for a total ride of 25 miles. Remember Highway 1 is
           heavily traveled in the summer so be careful.

Gegoka - Flathorn

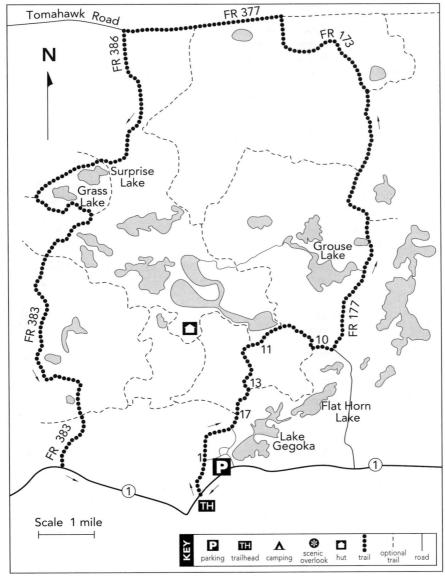

Maps are reproduced from USDA Forest Service Paul Witte, Cartographer (414) 297-3403.

Gooseberry Falls State Park
Two Harbors, MN   (218) 834-3855

Distance: 7.5 miles   **Trail:** Grassy ski trail, single-track
Ride time: 1-2 hours   **Rating:** Moderate

Access: Gooseberry Falls State Park is located thirty five miles north of Duluth, MN on U.S. Highway 61. There are three parking lots.

Gooseberry Falls State Park is part of the rugged Lake Superior shoreline. The Gooseberry River plunges over ancient lava flows to create some of the most majestic waterfalls in the region. Five spectacular waterfalls make Gooseberry Falls State Park a prime tourist attraction. Leave behind the masses of people who stop for a quick snapshot, and head for the more remote corners of the park.

0.0 mi.   At the north end of the old Interpretive Center start on the far left trail. Pedal along the mowed, grassy trail and listen to the roar of the falls to the left.

0.5 mi.   Turn left and continue on the ridge high above the river.

0.7 mi.   Dismount and hike down to "Fifth Fall." Here is where the Gooseberry River starts to dive over ancient lava flows towards Lake Superior. Back on the trail, pedal gradually uphill. At the top you are on a cliff that overlooks the rushing river. There will be a "do not enter" sign, but the signs are for skiing direction only. Turn right and pass a ski shelter and trail on your left.

1.2 mi.   Cross over snowmobile trail with orange diamond markings. Pedal .2 miles and a trail will join from the right.

1.8 mi.   Cross the snowmobile trail (for the second time) and several footbridges. This trail system sees little use in the summer so expect a good deal of solitude, perfect for bird watching or sunbathing.

2.1 mi.   Take the hiking trail to the right into the woods. Bump down the trail and cross one of many footbridges.

2.6 mi.   Veer left onto the hiking trail. The only place that it is legal to ride on the Superior Hiking Trail is within this park's boundaries. Pedal a short distance and stay to the left through the next interesection.

3.1 mi.   Note a trail entering from the left. Turn right and then left, stay on the Superior Hiking Trail. Pedal past the turn-off to Split Rock. The trail becomes faster and more rolling.

3.7 mi.   At the 5-way intersection, jog slightly left. Travel through several intersections, staying to the right.

4.2 mi.   Climb a long hill. You will be treated to a rustic log shelter and a spectacular view of the forested Sawtooth Mountains. They will not look much like mountains because they are some of the oldest in the world. Bump downhill for .5 miles back to the same 5-way intersection. Pass through the intersection onto the less traveled single-track, straight ahead. This is the most rolling part of the ride.

5.0 mi.   Turn onto "do no enter" trail to the left.

5.5 mi.   Return to the intersection with the Superior Hiking Trail. Ride to the left and pedal .3 miles. Make a left off of the hiking trail.

6.0 mi.   Turn left and climb up a small ridge to a nice overlook of the birch forest. Pedal over the rolling terrain for a mile to the trailhead.

Gooseberry Falls State Park

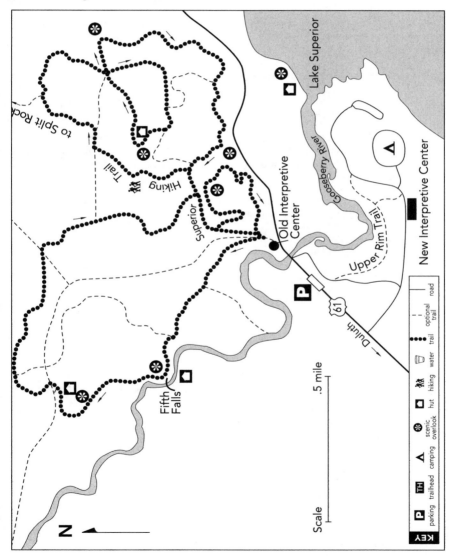

Copyright, State of Minnesota DNR, Reproduced with permission, Department of Natural Resources.
500 Lafayette Road St. Paul, Minnesota 55155.

Hidden Valley/Trezona Trail
Ely, MN   (218) 365-5489

Distance: 13 miles
Ride time: 2 hours

Trail: Grassy ski trails,
gravel roads, bike trails
Rating: Easy to Moderate

Access: Hwy 169 north to Ely. Take Central Ave. north for 2 blocks. Park in the gravel parking lot behind the Wilderness Outfitters store.

Ely is home to the International Wolf Center, and the gateway to the BWCA. It's one of the best places for camping, fishing, and unique shopping. A great time to visit Ely is during the famous Blueberry Fest in mid summer.

0.0 mi.   Start on the gravel trail, following the bike/ski signs heading east.

1.6 mi.   At the three-way intersection, turn right and cross a small road. Pedal easy on the winding paved path along a wet land.

2.3 mi.   Cross Hwy 169 at the Wolf Center and look for the road to the right. Make sure you visit the Wolf Center, it is famous for its research and re-introduction of the Timberwolf into the northwoods. Pedal up a big hill and roll down past the old ski jump area.

3.1 mi.   Feel free to park at the old ski building if you just want to ride the ski trail section. The trail starts through the gate.

4.0 mi.   Stay right and pedal through the woods and into a wildflower meadow. The ski trail will be marked with "no snowmobiling" signs.

4.5 mi.   Where the trail "Y"'s, stay left and pedal up and around a black spruce swamp. The trail to the right is always wet.

4.8 mi.   At the next "Y" stay right and cruise down the hill. You will cross several old logging roads.

5.9 mi.   Pedal on the main trail up to the abandoned ski jump. Fabulous views of the surrounding countryside and lakes.

6.0 mi.   Cruise down a long, winding trail. It is hard-packed and fast. Pop out by the old ski building and pedal back on the gravel road. There is a great view of Ely and the BWCA from here.

6.5 mi.   Pedal back on the gravel road past the Wolf Center and toward town.

7.7 mi.   Cross over the highway and onto the paved trail. You can continue around the lake or you can backtrack to the parking lot.

Hidden Valley/Trezona Trail

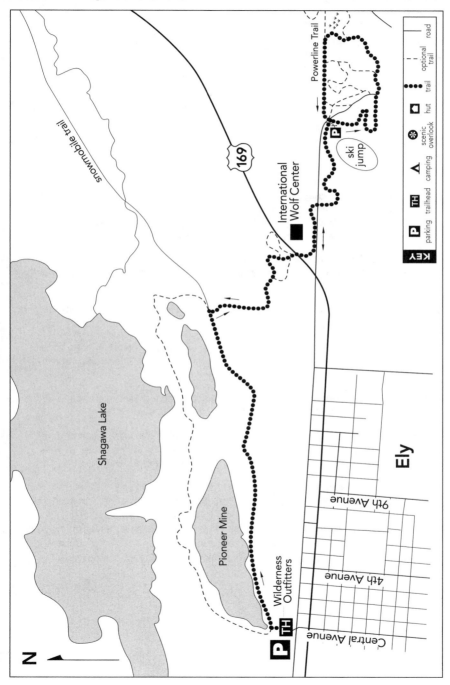

Lake Bemidji State Park
Bemidji, MN   (218) 755-3843

Distance: 6 miles
Ride time: 1 hour

Trail: Grassy ski trails
Rating: Easy

Access: Lake Bemidji State Park is located 1.7 miles off County Road 21, 5 miles north of Bemidji, MN. Entrance to the park is on Highway 20.

This state park offers visitors an enjoyable combination of Minnesota lake recreation and the experience of a northern forest. Lake Bemidji was named after the Chippewa Chief, Bemidji, whose tribe lived around the lake.

0.0 mi.   Park across from the Interpretive Center. Ride out the service road, north, through the campground. Take "the old logging road" trail at the end of the campground. Pedal until you come to the main paved road (20). Cross over to the other side. Here you will find a three-way intersection. Take the trail to the far left for the long loop.

0.7 mi.   For a challenging ride, take the left trail. Do not let this black diamond trail intimidate you. There are more downhills than uphills and the trail is smooth riding.

2.2 mi.   At the three-way junction, take the trail to the left. Pedal a short distance and come to a five-way intersection. Take trail number two (see map).

3.4 mi.   Come to a "Y" in the trail. Take the loop to the right. Pedal .5 miles through mixed forest and meadows. Go through the gate and "bush-wack" up onto FR #405.

4.0 mi.   Ride .25 miles and turn left. Pedal .5 miles. You will see an access road and the Pinewood Trail sign on the left.

4.7 mi.   Take this route back into the pines and through the woods. Small hills and gently rolling terrain make this an enjoyable ride for the novice as well the experienced rider. Come to the "Y", and turn right onto Pinewood Trail.

6.0 mi.   At the five-way intersection , turn left to take the Old Logging Road trail. This takes you to the Bog Interpretive Trail. Park your bikes at the bike rack and walk along the Bog Boardwalk. Learn to identify tamaracks and black spruce as well as a plethora of unusual plants that live only in a wet environment. After learning about all the plants and trees in a bog, hop back on your bike and pedal out to the trail. Turn left, crossing the paved road, and return to the campground.

Lake Bemidji State Park

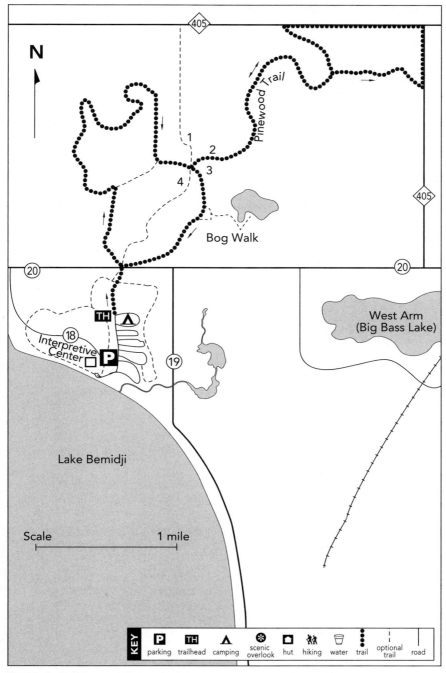

Laurentian Trail
Biwabik, MN   (800) 688-SNOW

Distance: 5.5 miles   **Trail:** Ski trails/snowmobile trails
Ride time: .75 - 1 hour   **Rating:** Easy to Moderate

Access: From Biwabik, MN take Highway 135 1.5 miles to County Road 138 north. Turn left and drive 3 miles north, following the Giants Ridge signs.

Ride the Wynne Creek Ridge above the Laurentian beaver flowage to see stands of 100 year old White Pines along with new growth areas. "The Ridge" is the home of the annual Labor Day Mountain Bike Fest. Allow several days to explore the more than 50 miles of off-road trails adjacent to Giants Ridge in the Superior National Forest. Look for major changes with the addition of a new golf course. Check the status of the trail before riding.

Laurentian snowmobile trail: Gravel base with moderate hills. Loose boulders, very few technical sections.

Laurentian ski trail: Grass base with easy to moderate downhills. Large protruding boulders that can be avoided.

Laurentian ski trail signs are faded and difficult to see. There are a few bike signs out on the course (but do not rely upon them). One is at the cutoff to the silver trail.

0.0 mi.   Ride your bike to the northeast corner of the paved parking lot. A small tar road to your right will bring you down a short, washed-out, gravel hill to the snowmobile intersection. Veer left onto the snowmobile trail. Follow this snowmobile trail over rolling hills that are mostly gravel based.

2.1 mi.   You will encounter the Taconite SnowmobileTrail. If you are feeling really adventurous take the Taconite Trail into the town of Babbitt, for a 40 mile out and back ride.

3.0 mi.   Here you will veer left onto the Laurentain Ski Trail, which is part of the Giants Ridge system. There will be a yellow map on a tree just after the gate on your right side.

          Follow the Laurentian Ski Trail which runs along a ridge overlooking Wynne Creek on your right. Can you spot the old mining cabin across the creek? Best to try this challenge late in the fall.

4.0 mi.   Continue straight ahead to finish the suggested loop. A grassy cutoff lets you access the Silver Trail. The Laurentian Ski Trail cuts through an area of old growth white pines.

4.3 mi.   Cross a grassy intersection that will connect to the Northern Lights loop. Cross the bridge. Climb several moderate hills and end up at the biathlon range intersection. Continue straight on the gravel road. Finish the 5.5 mile loop on the gravel road by riding straight through the remaining intersections and ending with a fun descent back to the main trailhead.

Laurentian Trail

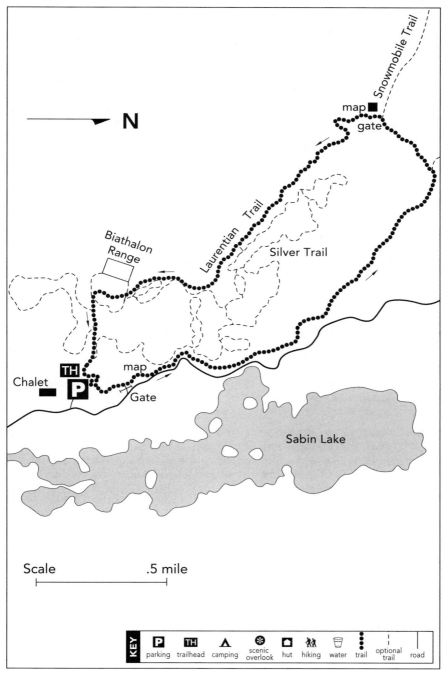

USGS 7.5 Series, Reproduced from Giants Ridge Resort.

Lee Mines Trail
Tower, MN   (218) 753-2301

Distance: 4 miles
Ride time: 1 hour

Trail: Two-track, short paved section
Rating: Easy to Intermediate

Access: Park behind the Tower High School. No amenities at the trailhead.

Most folks just travel through Tower on their way to someplace else; usually Ely. Stop in and visit the newly renovated depot museum. The ski trails in town are also very rideable if it has been dry. Big stands of red pines, several pretty overlooks of Lake Vermilion, and an old mining site make this ride unique.

0.0 mi.   The ride starts by climbing up a gravel, two track, through a stand of large red pines.

0.2 mi.   At the two-way intersection take a detour to the left for beautiful vistas.

0.9 mi.   Back on the main trail continue to climb up the double-track to the top. Stay left and head up to the Lake Vermilion overlook. Lake Vermilion is 40 miles long and is one of the largest lakes in Minnesota.

Ride back down from the overlook and follow the sign to Lee Mine- the trail can be dry and fast. You can catch air if you are not careful. Remember this is a multi-use trail and people may be hiking.

2.0 mi.   The Lee Mine is a small, clear, pond and marks the spot of the old iron mine. (An alternate ride can be taken to the Soudan Trail and to McKinley Park, which is on the edge of Lake Vermilion.)

From the mine fly down the trail. This is a fun, fast, rocky ride. The trail is technical enough to test your handling skills and fast enough to test your nerve. Remember to brake at the bottom before you fly out onto busy Hwy 1.

3.0 mi.   Pedal 1/8 mile along Hwy 1 and then cross over the road and hop on the paved Taconite Trail. Pedal east 1/2 mile back to the Information Center. The center is housed in a renovated, old railroad station; stop in for a chat and some treats. If you get lost they will help you find your way back to the parking lot behind the school.

Lee Mines Trail

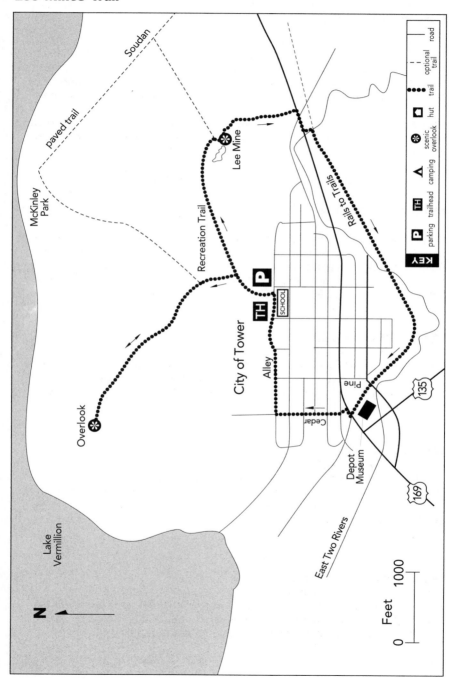

Lutsen Mountain Bike Park
Lutsen, MN   (218) 663-7281

The mountain bike park at Lutsen extends across four mountains and includes over 35 miles of trail. A combination of single-track, forest trails and open rock ledges provide several hours of interesting riding. Careful planning will match a route which best suits your riding ability. (Trail fee.)

Periodic stops along the way will allow you to discover a spectacular array of forest ecosystems along the north shore. The berries, flowers, forest and wildlife are an integral part of this sensational riding experience.

Lunches and beverages are available at the Mountain Top Deli.

Moose Mountain Trails: 4.5 miles
Intermediate and advanced riders only.
Access via gondola brings riders to an elevation 1,000 feet above Lake Superior. Steep descents. Rugged terrain. Open meadow areas abound in wildflowers. Raspberry picking is great in late July and August. Work roads provide a thrilling downhill ride. The ridgeline trail has a very technical single track section. The ledge rock in the Cascades area is a virtual riding playground.

Mystery Mountain Trails: 4.5 miles
Novice and intermediate riding.
Recommended for beginners, this short one mile loop takes riders on a trail to the Poplar river falls and old Lutsen homestead. Mystery mountain trail also connects with the Moose mountain trail system be a challenging section of single track.

Ullr Mountain Trail: 4.5 miles
Novice and intermediate riding.
This trail wraps around Ullr mountain in a slow, gradual climb, followed by a challenging downhill glide on the ski slopes of Ullr mountain. Take a moment to enjoy the overlook of the marshland above the Poplar river falls. Keep a close eye for moose, otter and a variety of waterfowl. (This trail has a few wet, marshy sections.)

Eagle Mountain Trail: 2 miles
Intermediate and advances riders only.
This is a straight forward, no frills, uphill/downhill trail. A steep ascent to the top of Eagle mountain. A quick, technical descent back down. Look for wild strawberries as an energy booster in early July-they're terrific!

Lutsen Mountain Bike Park

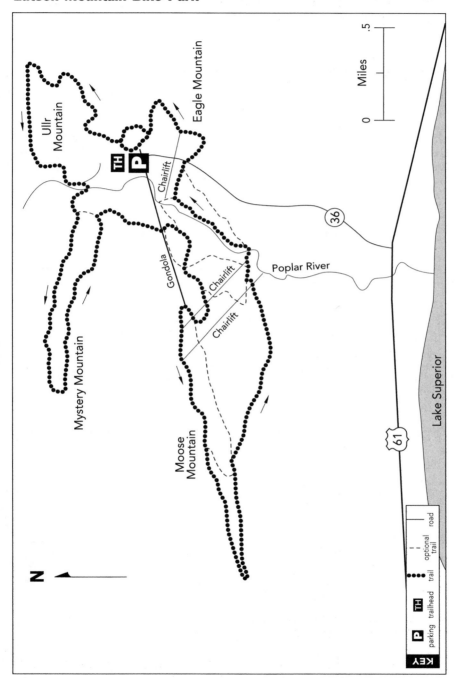

McCarthy Beach State Park
Hibbing, MN   (218) 254-2411

Distance: 15.5 miles
Ride time: 2-3 hours

Trail: Grassy double and single-track
Rating: Moderate

Access: From Hibbing, MN take Highway 169 north to County Road 5. Follow this county road 15 miles north to the park.

McCarthy Beach State Park is situated between Sturgeon Lake and Side Lake. The attraction for summer visitors here is usually water recreation. Leave the crowd at the beach and head off into the hills of the park, where all trails are open for riding. The deeply wooded trails follow the contour of the ridge tops and valleys that were shaped by the last retreating glacier. The Big Hole Loop encircles the top of a deep depression caused when a large ice-block was left to melt.

0.0 mi.   Park at the visitors' lot and pedal to the north end of the campground. Ride half a mile and pick up the Pickerel Lake/Red Top Trail loop.

1.2 mi.   The trail merges with a forest road. Follow the road to the right for a short distance. Look for the sign to the Pickerel Trail Loop. Turn left onto a small footpath for a wonderful rolling ride around the lake.

1.3 mi.   At jct. 3, near the north end of the lake, stay right to continue the loop. The narrow single-track with encroaching brush along the lake makes you feel like you are in the BWCA.

2.3 mi.   To continue the suggested ride, cross over a small footbridge. This is a potentially wet area. The trail "Y's", with private property to the left.

2.8 mi.   Complete the Pickerel Lake Loop. Head up the road to jct. 1. Turn right at the "T" in the road and ride a quarter mile. Take a left onto Ridge Trail. Immediately to your right will be a hiking trail. Stay on the main trail. The gently rolling trail will be carpeted with pine needles. At the top of a rise is a rustic shelter tucked into a stand of huge red pines. This is a nice picnic area with glimpses of Sturgeon Lake.

4.1 mi.   A narrow hiking trail on the right will be marked Red Top (jct. 11). Use this trail as a short cut to the inner loop.

5.8 mi.   Roll downhill to jct. 13 and a shelter. Turn right onto Taconite Trail.

7.5 mi.   Pedal a couple miles on Taconite Trail until you come to FR 501. Turn right and pedal a short distance on the road. Turn right into the woods. Pick up Red Top Trail to the right. Proceed .25 miles and jog right at jct. 7. Pass jct. 8. Red Top Trail cruises along the top of an old moraine, an ancient glacier formation made up of debris left by a retreating ice sheet.

8.3 mi.   Pass jct. 9. At an unmarked intersection, jog left down onto the ski trail. There will be a climb on either route.

Continued on page 42

McCarthy Beach State Park

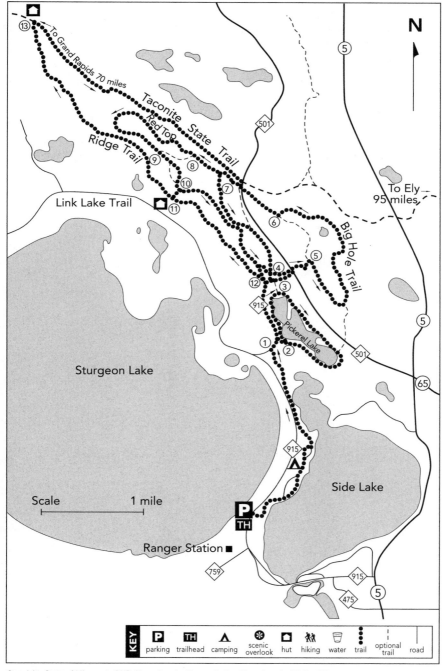

Copyright, State of Minnesota DNR, Reproduced with permission, Department of Natural Resources.
500 Lafayette Road St. Paul, Minnesota 55155.

9.3 mi. At the top of the hill the trails join Red Top Trail (jct. 10). Turn left onto the trail marked "do not enter" (ski direction). This trail will parallel the Ridge Trail at the bottom of the valley.

10.0 mi. Stay left through the unmarked intersections. Ride through jct. 4 and cross the road onto Big Hole loop.

10.5 mi. Turn right at jct. 5 and coast downhill to a "Y." Turn left. Ride around the top of a deep basin called Big Hole, a glacial depression left during the last ice age.

12.2 mi. Turn right at jct. 6 to leave Big Hole trail. Cross the road. Turn left at jct. 7. There is a big downhill near the end of this leg. Take the forest road to your right and head back to the campground.

See, Biff, I told you it pays to take care of your bike!

Movil Maze
Bemidji, MN   (218) 751-3456

Distance: 6.4 miles
Ride time: 1.5-2 hours

Trail: Single track and grassy ski trails
Rating: Moderate to Advanced

Access: The Movil Maze trails are located 8 miles north of Bemidji, on US Hwy 71. West on County Road 45 for one mile. Look for ski signs.

Be careful! People have been known to get lost in this county forest, thus the name "The Maze". Keep track of where you are with a map, the ski trails are not usually labeled in the summer. You can tell if you are on a ski trail by the blue diamond markers. The orange markers indicate snowmobile trails.

0.0 mi.	Begin the trail in the parking lot. Look for the orange snowmobile marker to the right of the ski trail. The snowmobile trail may have debris to watch out for. This also means it is a narrower corridor, hard-packed and fast.
1.1 mi.	Come to the only big mucky part of the ride. Expect to get your feet wet even during dry seasons.
1.5 mi.	Pass through a four-way intersection. The trail requires some challenging climbing.
1.8 mi.	Pedal past a trail on your left and then climb a long steep hill up to a ridge for a fantastic peek at Lake Movil. If you have had your fill of climbing, roll <u>down</u> the hill to take a dip in the lake. Back at the top, continue to the left through a stand of aspens. Roll down through beautiful mature red pines and cross over an old plank bridge.
2.8 mi.	Roll into an open meadow. Continue straight on the trail. You will pass several trails on your left. Either of these trails can take you to the interior loops of the Movil Maze.
3.3 mi.	Turn off the snowmobile trail and onto the Movil Maze ski trail. Pedal through a stand of aspens and through a low area that may be wet.
3.4 mi.	At the three-way jct. go right for the outside loop. Look for the cedar bog on your left.
4.1 mi.	You will find yourself at a four-way intersection. There are several old logging roads that have been incorporated into the ski trails.
4.2 mi.	At this junction you will turn right. The terrain is a little soft here, but only for a short distance.
4.6 mi.	Ride past an adjoining spur to your right. Here the trail becomes more rolling. Fast descents and easy climbs make you hoot.
5.1 mi.	Climb a hill to a three-way intersection. Stay to the right and pedal around the outside loop. There will be several small trails splitting off the main trail. Stay on the main trail. Remember, it's not called the "Maze" for nothing.

5.7 mi.   Stay to the right. You are back at the beginning of the small loop. Pedal .1 miles past a trail to your left.

6.0 mi.   Three-way jct. stay to the right. Pedal on rolling trails, through maples, aspens and birch.

6.2 mi.   Cross over ski trailhead area and pedal .2 miles back to the parking lot.

Movil Maze

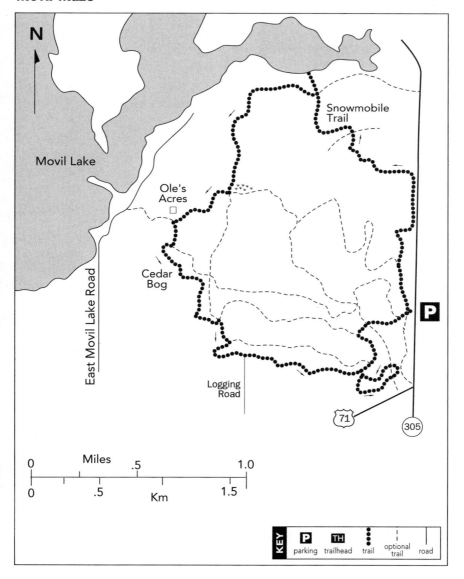

Pincushion Mountain
Grand Marais, MN   (218) 387-1750

Distance: 6 miles
Ride time: 1.5 - 2 hours

Trail: Single-track loop
Rating: Moderate

Access: The Pincushion Mountain Ski Area is located 2 miles north of Grand Marais, MN on the Gunflint Trail (Co. Rd. 12). The parking area is located on the east side of the Gunflint Trail. Look for the cross country ski signs.

It would be hard to find a bad trail on a perfect autumn day; crisp air with full sun, no bugs and the leaves at peak color. The views of Grand Marais and Lake Superior are a bonus to this trail system.

0.0 mi.   15 miles of interconnecting trails allow for a variety of loops. Pedal up the trail. At the five-way intersection turn right. This 1km loop is soft, but has no steep hills.

0.6 mi.   Turn right at this intersection, you will be riding the ski trails backwards on this part of the loop.

1.0 mi.   The trail forks. Take the trail to the right. Expect mud, water and hikers. Cross several foot bridges.

1.4 mi.   There will be trails to the left, continue forward on trail. Notice a small trail paralleling the main trail. Turn left for the shortcut trail.

2.2 mi.   Crank to the top of the hill. There is a marker and a foot trail to the top of Pincushion Mountain. For a great side trip, hike a quarter mile up onto a rocky bluff for the most spectacular panoramic overview of Lake Superior and the Superior National Forest. Standing at this vantage point you can see how Grand Marais got its name. The Native Americans called it the "Big Pond."

2.5 mi.   Pedal .5 miles through beautiful birch and aspen forest to where the Superior Hiking Trail splits off to the north. Biking is not allowed on the Superior Hiking Trail. Pedal above the ravine cut by Devils Track River. The river was used by loggers at the turn of the century, which was not an easy feat considering the river has many waterfalls and rapids.

3.4 mi.   Come to a three-way intersection. Turn right for several strenuous hill climbs and technical descents.

3.7 mi.   Climb along the hill to a three-way junction. Turn right to continue on the outer loop with near hairpin turns and lots of ups and downs.

4.0 mi.   At large intersection turn right and climb long hill following the Pincushion Bed and Breakfast signs. Turn right onto a rugged little single-track trail with many exposed roots. Cross over dirt road.

4.5 mi.   Cruise down a long hill and cross a footbridge. Beware that at the bottom of each hill is usually a plank bridge with a lip.

5.2 mi.   Turn right onto a less traveled trail at a three-way intersection, (not the "do not enter"). Bump along the trail .8 miles to the trailhead.

Pincushion Mountain

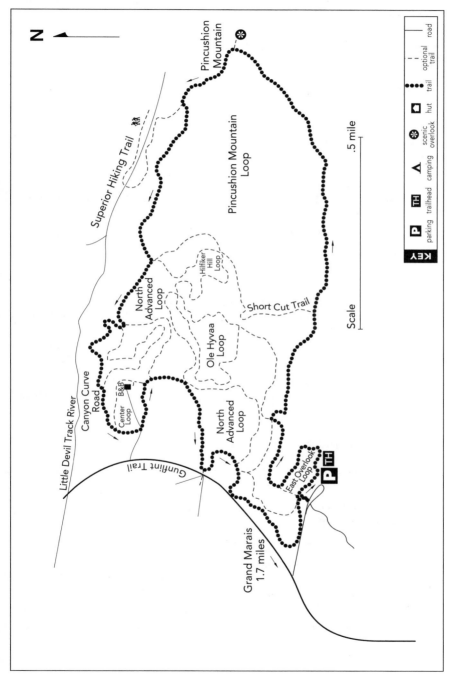

Maps are reproduced from USDA Forest Service Paul Witte, Cartographer (414) 297-3403.

Scenic State Park
Big Fork, MN   (218) 743-3362

Distance: 18 total miles
Ride time: 2-4 hours

Trail: Ski/hiking trails
Rating: Easy to Moderate

Access: From Big Fork, MN drive 7 miles east on County Road 7. A Minnesota State Park sticker is required.

Ancient receding glaciers left ridges, depressions, and soil deposits that make up the rolling terrain that is perfect for mountain biking. The park has something to offer everyone, from nesting ospreys to glacial eskers to world-class fishing.

0.0 mi.	Park behind the ranger station. This is the pivot point for two connecting loops and can be used as a "bail out point." Pedal through the campground above Coon Lake.
0.1 mi.	The trail crosses a paved road and heads into the woods. The double-track is smooth and relatively flat. Pedal through a beautiful mixed forest.
2.2 mi.	You will notice a ski trail joins from the right. Ride a quarter mile to where the trail splits. Stay to the right.
2.8 mi.	Pedal past the sign for the fire tower. There are several backcountry campsites off this trail. If you want privacy with a beautiful view of Pine Lake, this is the spot to camp. (Check with the ranger on availability.)
3.0 mi.	Pass the second backcountry site. Turn right onto the ski trail. The trail marks the northern border of the park. This area is one of two old growth areas in the park. You will find some of the largest and oldest red and white pines in the state. This old growth area has little undergrowth so you can see deep into the forest.
4.0 mi.	Follow the double-track past several snowmobile spurs on the left. Turn right onto the single-track ski trail and take another right at the bottom of a gradual downhill. The terrain here is flat until you approach the fire tower. Climb the sharp incline. You will find an old foundation complete with standing stone chimney and functional hand pump; the remains of an old ranger cabin.
	Climb the tower for a spectacular view of Chippewa National Forest and Coon Lake. Take a left at the fire tower.
5.7 mi.	The ski trail will merge from the right. Look out for hikers and be courteous.
6.4 mi.	Cross over the park road and into Lodge Campground. Pedal through the campground, pass the lodge, and pick up a small maintenance road. Pedal back to the ranger station, backtracking along Coon Lake and through Chase Point Campground.
7.5 mi.	Grab a soda (there are machines behind the ranger station) and take a break. This is the end of the first loop which is the easiest riding in the park.

Continued on page 50

Scenic State Park

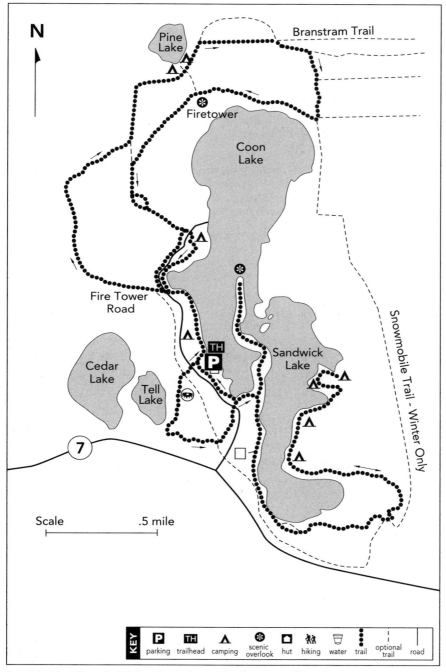

N

Branstram Trail

Pine Lake

Firetower

Coon Lake

Fire Tower Road

Cedar Lake

Tell Lake

Sandwick Lake

Snowmobile Trail - Winter Only

7

Scale .5 mile

KEY — P parking — TH trailhead — ▲ camping — ✳ scenic overlook — ▢ hut — 🏃 hiking — 🪣 water — ● trail — optional trail — road

The ride becomes more rugged with single-track and longer out and back sections of trail. The 1 mile loop begins directly across the road from the ranger station. Do not ride this trail when the park is busy.

There is a steep downhill that crosses a boardwalk. Pedal along a small ridge above Tell Lake. If you are quiet you may spot nesting ospreys. Ospreys return to the same nesting sites each year.

8.3 mi.   Pedal through mostly birch and aspen forest. Cross over snowmobile trail. Pedal .25 miles and cross over a paved access road and turn right. Take a left onto Chase Point trail.

This trail is actually on a glacial esker, a long ridge of land formed by deposits from a river tunnel beneath a glacier. Here you are amid stands of white cedar, balsam fir and red pine, Minnesota's state tree. From the point is a beautiful view of Coon Lake. If the park is busy avoid this popular hiking area.

10.7 mi.   Backtrack on Chase Point trail and turn left at the first intersection. Ride on an old paved road .25 miles and turn left onto the ski trail. Ride down close to the shore of Sandwick lake. The trail splits. Regardless of which trail you choose you will have to grunt up the hill. Roll up and down numerous hills through tight turns for 1.3 miles

12.0 mi.   Turn left for .25 miles on a logging road. At the ski trail turn left. This is a beautiful ride along Sandwick Lake through an old growth forest. You will find several excellent backcountry camping sites with wonderful views of the lake. Bring your swimsuit and fishing pole.

14.5 mi.   There is a ski shelter at the very end of the trail that is usually stocked with a supply of firewood. This is a nice lunch spot.

Double back on the same trail. Come to the main park road. Finish the loop by taking the hiking trail straight ahead. Cross a long boardwalk and climb a short steep hill. You will be behind the ranger station.

And you thought the midwest was flat...

Silver Trail
Biwabik, MN   (800) 688-SNOW

Distance: 6.2 miles   **Trail:** Rolling ski trails
Ride time: 1-1.5 hours   **Rating:** Moderate to Advanced

Access: From Biwabik, MN take Highway 135 1.5 miles to County Road 138 north. Turn left and drive 3 miles following the Giants Ridge signs.

Giants Ridge is a great area that supports mountain biking on its world-class cross country ski trails. In addition there are over 50 miles of off-road trails adjacent to Giants Ridge in the Superior National Forest. Look for major changes with the addition of a new golf course. Check the status of the trail before riding. (Trail Fee)

0.0 mi.   The Silver Trail starts north of the ski chalet. The trail marker is located on the light standard on the right side of the trail.

0.6 mi   You will begin a series of three short, steep hills.

1.0 mi.   Stay to your right for the suggested loop. Notice the 3.5K cutoff to the left. Pedal .4 miles for a nice view of Lake Sabin.

1.5 mi.   Veer right and follow a short, challenging loop that merges onto the main trail.

1.8 mi.   Pedal to the right past the 5K, 6.5K and 7.5K cutoffs.

4.2 mi.   Follow the Silver Trail. The Laurentian Trail is to the right. Pass several trails that join from the left.

4.5 mi.   The 3.5K cutoff rejoins the main trail here.

4.7 mi.   Ride on the Silver Trail through the next three intersections. Thick woods and the rolling terrain make this area mountain biking heaven.

5.2 mi.   Follow the Silver Trail up a short, steep hill, down under a bridge, and straight through an intersection. You will encounter several grassy cutoffs to the left. Stay on the Silver Trail.

5.6 mi.   Turn left at the chalet and biathlon sign. Follow this trail down a gradual descent. Look for the Silver Trail 9km cutoff on your right.

6.2 mi.   Cross the gravel road and veer to the right staying on Silver Trail. This will be a gradual descent back to the trailhead.

Silver Trail

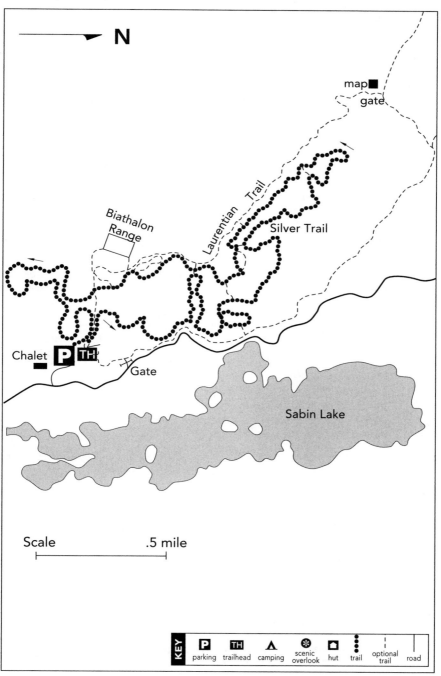

USGS 7.5 Series, Reproduced from Giants Ridge Resort.

Split Rock State Park
Two Harbors, MN   (218) 226-3065

Distance: 7 miles   **Trail:** Well maintained grass or gravel trails
Ride time: 1-2 hours   **Rating:** Moderate

Access: The Split Rock State Park is located twenty miles north of Two Harbors, MN on U.S. Hwy 61. A Minnesota State Park sticker is required to enter the park.

Split Rock State Park lies on the rocky, rugged, Lake Superior shoreline where some of the world's oldest mountains melt into the world's largest freshwater lake. Much Great Lakes history surrounds the lighthouse which is the "most photographed lighthouse in the world."

0.0 mi.   Park at the trail center located down the hill from the ranger station. Pick up the walking trail to the right of the large picnic shelter. Remember, this is a busy park and the foot trails nearest the lighthouse will be the most traveled. You will also be pedaling past several backcountry campsites,...so be courteous!

0.5 mi.   Pass the bathhouse. The trail winds into the woods towards the lake. Follow hiking club signs. Most intersections will be marked with "you are here" signs.

0.9 mi   Climb the hill to the right onto the "Day Hill Trail." You will come to a trail marked "Top of the Day." Hike a quarter mile to the top of a rocky outcropping for an incredible view of the lighthouse and the rugged shoreline of Lake Superior.

1.1 mi.   Tear yourself away from the view (there will be more) and pedal to the next intersection. Turn right and cross over Highway 61. Be careful, this is heavily traveled. Pick up the trail on the other side. The trail west of the highway is relatively flat, but exposed roots and rocks, coupled with a few boggy areas, make this loop a little more difficult.

2.0mi.   Cross over footbridge and climb a short hill to the left. The "Superior Hiking Trail" will split to the right. (Mountain biking is not allowed.)

2.5 mi.   Pedal through a small creek and climb a second short hill. This bumpy trail will split. If you want to avoid the challenging climb, take the short cut.

2.9 mi.   The trail will hairpin at the top of a very steep pitch with loose rock. When you stop at the top for a breather, take in the beautiful view of Lake Superior. Follow the hairpin and go down the hill. Be careful here there are half buried timbers laid across the trail.

3.3 mi.   The shortcut will join the trail from the left. Bump down the trail and cross back over Highway 61. Ride to the right on old blacktop for .2 miles. Pick up the trail to the left near the water.

3.5 mi.   Catch glimpses of the lake as you pedal along a small ridge. Cruise along the scenic trail for access to several secluded beaches. It will take a hardy soul

Continued on page 56

Split Rock State Park

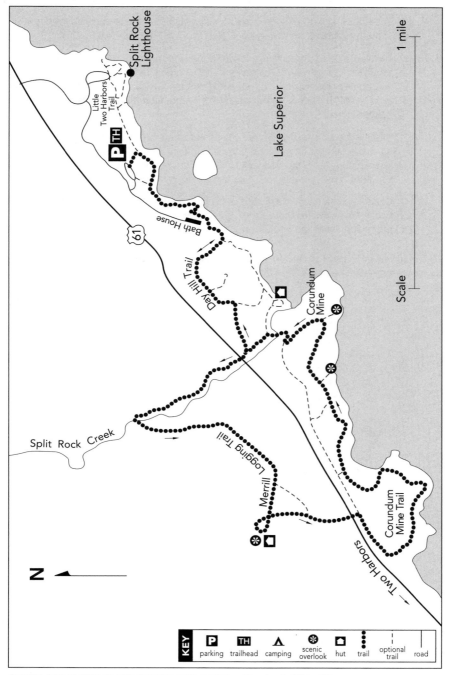

KEY — P parking · TH trailhead · ▲ camping · ✳ scenic overlook · ◻ hut · ⦙ trail · optional trail · road

and a thick skin to swim in Lake Superior. Numerous outcroppings are prime spots for relaxing, sunbathing and picnics.

5.0 mi. Turn left at the intersection away from the lake; pedal .2 miles. The foot trail to the right will lead you to remnants of the "Corundum Mine," a material used as an abrasive. Not much is known about this mine except that it was in operation from 1901-1910 until they discovered that the material they were mining was not corundum!

5.6 mi. Cross a footbridge and turn left. Climb out of a small ravine towards Highway 61 and a familiar intersection. Ride to the right. You will come to an intersection where the trail looks like nice single-track. Stay to the left unless you want to be carrying your bike up and down hundreds of stairs!!

Continue back to the trailhead staying to the left. There is a beautiful rock beach below the lighthouse that is great for agate hunting, sunbathing and a refreshing dip at the end of a hot ride.

Recommendation: Reserve a scenic backcountry campsite right on Lake Superior. This will give you an opportunity to do day rides in both Gooseberry Falls and Split Rock.

Flies have perfected the art of drafting!

Whitefish Lake
Tofte, MN   (218) 387-1750

Distance: 20 miles
Ride time: 3-4 hours

Trail: Loop with rocky double-track
Rating: Moderate

Access: Whitefish Lake is located northwest of Tofte, MN. Take FR 343 north to FR 166. Take a left on 166 to FR 346. Take 346 north to FR 170. Follow 170 left to north FR 357. Park at the Whitefish Lake boat landing.

Whitefish Lake sits deep in the Arrowhead Region of Cook County. The fall color tour in the Arrowhead Region encompasses this old forest road.

0.0 mi.   Ride out to FR 357 and continue riding to the right. This turns into FR 348; the road will become more narrow and rocky as it winds towards Bone Lake. The trail will skirt several ponds and marshes. You will not actually see Whitefish Lake except at the beginning of the ride.

5.0 mi.   Pedal along the trail to Bone Lake, a pristine trout lake. It has been said that you can pull in some big ones right from the shore, so make sure you pack a picnic lunch and your fishing pole.

8.0 mi.   Cross small creek and pedal up the hill away from the lake. From here the trail becomes more rolling with a generally uphill terrain. Maples, aspen and birch and several large boulders line the trail. There is a potential for puddles if it has been wet. Several bull moose have been seen along this trail.

10.0 mi.   Pedal past another beaver pond and moose bog and cross several shallow creeks. Parts of the trail will become flat and smooth. Long sections of rocky areas will test your bike handling skills.

14.0 mi.   The two-track improves, becoming less rough and rocky.

15.5 mi.   At FR 170, turn right and ride on the main dirt road 1 mile.

16.5 mi.   Turn right onto the two-track FR 1226 (look for a bike marker). This rocky, hard-packed, two-track road takes you over the Cross River and back to the south side of Whitefish Lake. When you hit a "T" in the road take a right onto FR 357 back to the boatlanding parking area.

Whitefish Lake

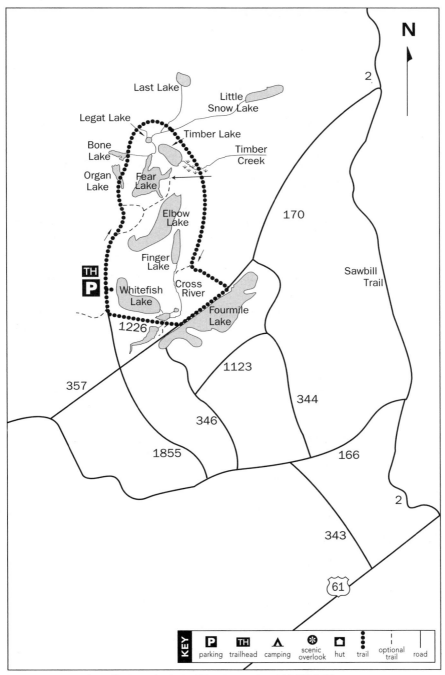

Maps are reproduced from USDA Forest Service Paul Witte, Cartographer (414) 297-3403.

Wynne Lake Overlook
Biwabik, MN   (800)-688-SNOW

Distance: 10 miles
Ride time: 2-3 hours

Trail: Loop on ski & snowmobile trails
Rating: Moderate

Access: From Biwabik, MN take Highway 135 1.5 miles to County Road 138 north. Turn left and drive 3 miles following the Giants Ridge signs.

The Wynne Lake trail climbs to an overlook of Embarrass Lake, Sabin Lake, Wynne Lake and the Superior National Forest. Few areas can surpass this spot for its beauty. Ride "The Ridge," where world-class cross country ski trails make for some of the best fat-tire trails in the Midwest. Allow several days to explore the more than 50 miles of off-road trails adjacent to Giants Ridge in the Superior National Forest. Giants Ridge is the home of the annual Labor Day Mountain Bike Fest.

0.0 mi.   Pedal South of the ski chalet along the base of the ski hills past the chairlifts. Pick up the Bronze and Oslo ski trail as it enters the woods. The trail is smooth and relatively flat at the beginning.

0.6 mi.   At the first "Y" stay to the left. You will climb a little more.

1.5 mi.   The Bronze and Oslo trails split to the left. Cruise down the hill and follow Oslo trail signs.

2.7 mi.   You will come to a rocky road. Take the road to the left and cross over County Road 138. At the top of the hill take the first trail to the right and jog right onto the snowmobile trail. The trail will cross a wooden bridge over a channel of water between Wynne and Embarrass Mine Lakes.

4.0 mi.   Take a small gravel road to the left. Here you can access Embarrass Mine Lake. This is an old iron ore pit that has been reclaimed as a recreational lake. Note the crystal clear water. Pedal up the road .5 miles to a 5-way intersection. Take trail number three (see map).

4.5 mi.   Pedal up a moderate incline. The two-track will be a little rocky with several washed out areas. You are acutally riding up a 300' pile of debris left over from iron ore mining.

5.1 mi.   At the top of the hill take the first grassy spur to the left for a great panoramic view of Wynne Lake and the Superior National Forest. You can see 40 miles on a clear day.

5.6 mi.   Cruise back down to the 5-way intersection and climb up trail number one (see map). This will lead you to the top of another hill and a great view of Embarrass Mine Lake.

6.1 mi.   Double back on the road to the snowmobile trail that you came on. Cross back over the wooden bridge and climb the hill to the gravel road. Take the road to the right and then turn onto the snowmobile trail to the left. You will pedal through the woods along Wynne Lake while paralleling Rd. 138.

9.5 mi.   At the Laurentian Village cross the road to Giants Ridge, and pedal back along the ski lifts to the parking lot.

Wynne Lake Overlook

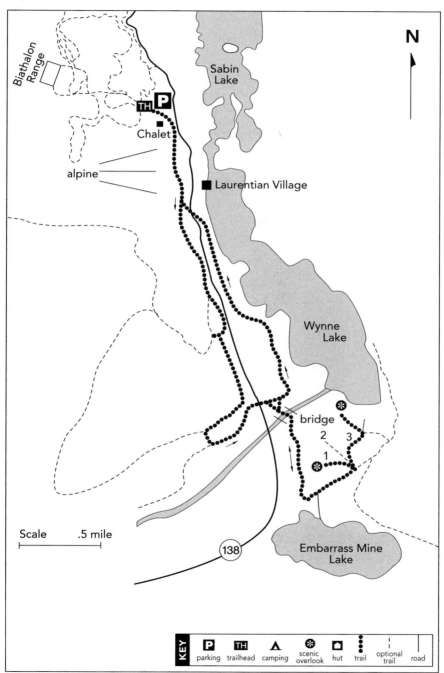

Scale   .5 mile

KEY — **P** parking   **TH** trailhead   **▲** camping   **✱** scenic overlook   **◻** hut   **⋮** trail   optional trail   road

USGS 7.5 Series, Reproduced from Giants Ridge Resort.

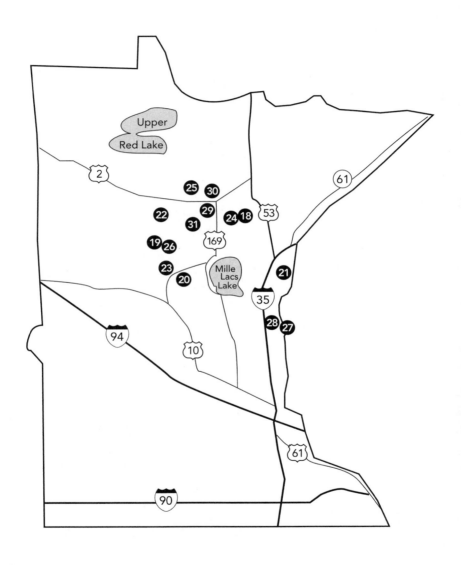

The North Country Guide to
Mountain Biking

SECTION 2

Central Minnesota

18 Continental Divide Trail

19 Cut Lake Trail

20 French Rapids Trail

21 Jay Cooke State Park

22 Paul Bunyan State Forest

23 Pillsbury State Forest

24 Savanna Portage State Park

25 Simpson Creek

26 Spider Lake Trail

27 St. Croix State Forest

28 St. Croix State Park

29 Sugar Hills Trail

30 Suomi Hill Trail

31 Washburn Lake Trail

Continental Divide Trail
McGregor, MN   (218) 426-3271

Distance: 10 miles
Ride time: 2-3 hours

Trail: loop: single-track, dirt road
Rating: Moderate

Access: Savanna Portage State Park is located 50 miles west of Duluth, MN or 135 miles north of the Twin Cities. Take Highway 65 north. Turn right at County Road 14 and follow it 10 miles to the park. To enter the park you need a Minnesota State Park sticker.

French voyagers, with their colorful outfits and folksongs, first penetrated this region in 1763. Voyagers and fur traders portaged their canoes from the East to the West Savanna River, a vital link across the Continental Divide between the St. Louis and Mississippi Rivers. This grueling, 6 mile portage took an average of five days under heavy loads. Today, the 15,000 acres of hardwood forests that define the park provide refuge for a variety of wildlife and a glimpse into our rich past.

0.0 mi. Park at the boat launch. Ride the road that exits the parking lot to the left. Enter the first campground loop to the left. Find the trail at campsite #20. The 2 mile loop around Lake Shumway is a gently undulating trail that allows for sightseeing while encircling the lake. The loop ends back at the boat launch parking area.

2.0 mi. Ride away from the lake. Take the trail to the right. At the first intersection stay to the right. Look for the Wolf Lake-Continental Divide signs.

2.3 mi. Take the trail labeled Wolf Lake-Continental Divide at jct. 10.

2.7 mi. Turn right at a large intersection. You are on a 1.2 mile out and back trail to Wolf Lake. This is a beautiful ride that ends at a secluded backcountry campsite! Watchout for a long, tricky section of primitive boardwalk.

3.9 mi. Climb the hill to your right. You are riding on the Continental Divide. On one side the water flows via Lake Superior to the Atlantic Ocean, on the other side it flows via the Mississippi River to the Gulf of Mexico. Climb up the trail to another backcountry campsite and a beautiful overview of Wolf Lake.

5.7 mi. Take a left onto the dirt road and cruise down the hill. Stay on the road past the Savanna Portage historical marker.

6.9 mi. Turn right and climb a short, steep, grassy hill. This trail skirts private land on the west. There is a nice overlook of the West Savanna River.

7.8 mi. Take a right at the dirt road, then turn left at the ranger station. Follow the road to trail "A." The first part of this trail is flat, but boggy. The second half contains short steep climbs and passes another backcountry campsite before returning to the dirt road.

9.4 mi. Turn left onto the dirt road and follow it back to the boat launch parking area.

RECOMMENDATIONS: Bring your packs and ride into one of three backcountry campsites to spend the night. Permits are required; please check in at the ranger station.

Continental Divide Trail

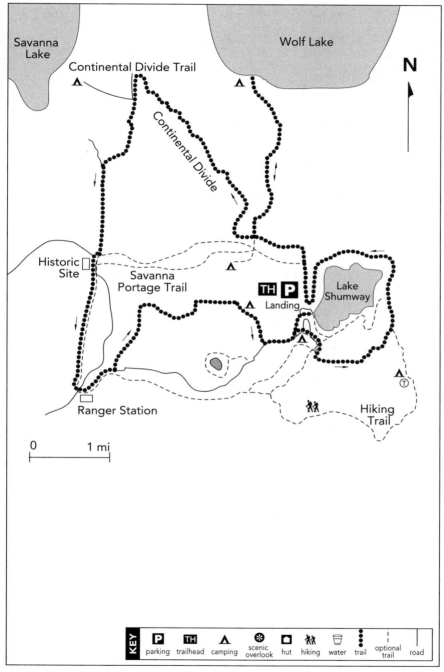

Cut Lake
Backus, MN   (218) 947-3232

Distance: 7 miles   **Trail:** Dirt two-track
Ride Time: 1.5 hours   **Rating:** Easy to Intermediate

Access: The trail is located 11 miles west of Pine River on County Highway 2. Look for the Cut Lake trails on the north side of Hwy. 2.

Cut Lake sits in the Foothills State Forest with over 43,000 acres in central Cass County. These trails are on land formed from glacial activity and covered in forests of red, white and jack pines as well as oak, maple, basswood and spruce. This network of old logging roads and ski trails is marked for mountain biking and there is a map at the trailhead.

0.0 mi.   Pedal 1/2 mile on rolling grassy trails.

0.5 mi.   Orioles, scarlet tanagers and cardinals scatter as you pedal straight ahead for the outside loop.

0.7 mi.   Ride the teardrop loop for an additional 1/2 mile.

1.4 mi.   Stay right for the outside loop. Several rolling hills carry you past a lake on your right.

2.7 mi.   Pedal to "T" intersection. Deer Lake will be right in front of you. Take the right-hand trail to go around Deer Lake.

2.8 mi.   Cross over a dirt road (boat launch). This trail is a black diamond, but don't let that scare you it's not as bad as you think.

3.3 mi.   Pedal up the hill to a ski shelter for a view of the lake. We spotted a porcupine napping in the sun and decided to skip the view.

3.7 mi.   At the "Y" intersection you can go onto the inner trails for a more moderate ride through the hardwoods and along several small lakes. Or follow the trail to the right and take the outer loop.

The outer trail is more wet and is considered a black diamond trail. Expect to climb and descend steep hills.

4.0 mi.   Pass several small lakes on your right.

6.0 mi.   The trail will cross over an old logging trail.

6.6 mi.   At the "T" turn right and pedal .3 miles to the parking lot for a total of 7 miles.

Cut Lake

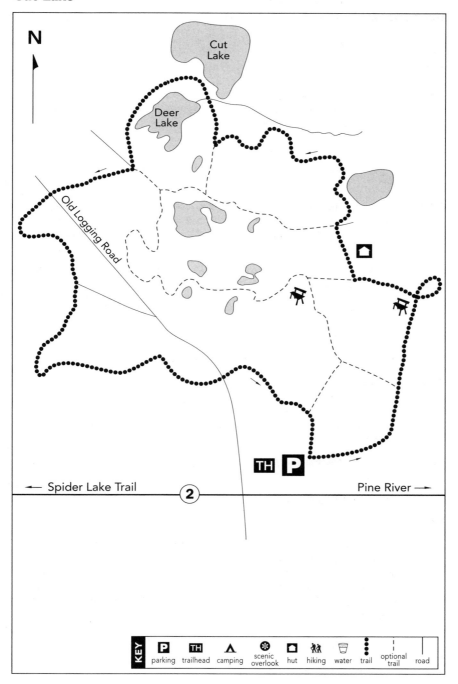

French Rapids Trail
Brainerd, MN　(218) 829-2838

Distance: 7.5 miles (10 total)　　　**Trail:**　Rolling, hard-packed, ski trails
Ride time: 1-2 hours　　　　　　　**Rating:**　Moderate to Advanced

Access:　From Brainerd, MN go northeast on Highway 210. Turn left at the airport exit on County Road 142 . Drive 2.5 miles. Take a second unmarked left. The road dead-ends at the trailhead.

Cruising the hilly terrain along the mighty Mississippi on your bike is a fabulous adventure and a great workout. The French Rapids Cross Country Ski Area is ideal for mountain biking in spring, summer or fall.

0.0 mi.　Park where the road dead-ends and pedal around the gate up the Portage Trail. Climb .3 miles and ride past the first intersection. Several small ponds on the right and the Mississippi on the left squeeze you up onto a narrow ridge.

0.8 mi.　Pedal along the river through the next intersection. A mixed forest of pine, birch and aspen canopy the trail. Watch out for a few sandy sections. Steep climbs with loose rock and gravel make this a challenging ride.

2.0 mi.　Turn left onto a logging road. This is the East River Loop. Expect wider trails, or roads wide enough to accommodate logging trucks for a short distance.

2.6 mi.　The trail splits at the top of a small hill. The less traveled East River trail is marked to the right. The trail closely follows the river.

3.5 mi.　The trail "Y's" under the canopy of towering white pines. Veer right for an overlook of the river. This knoll above a bend in the river, carpeted with pine needles, makes a perfect picnic spot. Pedal back to the main trail and veer right. Pass the East River Trail intersection and continue beyond a recent clear-cut area.

4.9 mi.　The trail is not well marked, so look closely for the Shelter Trail in the woods to the right.

5.5 mi.　Follow the trail left onto the Einers Run. The rolling trail is less sandy.

6.5 mi.　Stay left on Einers Run.

6.8 mi.　Pedal through heavily wooded areas of oak, pine, birch and aspen. Notice the snowmobile trail joining from the left. Turn right to Debbie's Hill. Climb a short hill and make a thrilling descent down the other side. Beware of washed-out areas and a few sandy pockets. Continue through the next two intersections and turn left at the third intersection. Turn left onto Portage Trail back to the trailhead.

French Rapids Trail

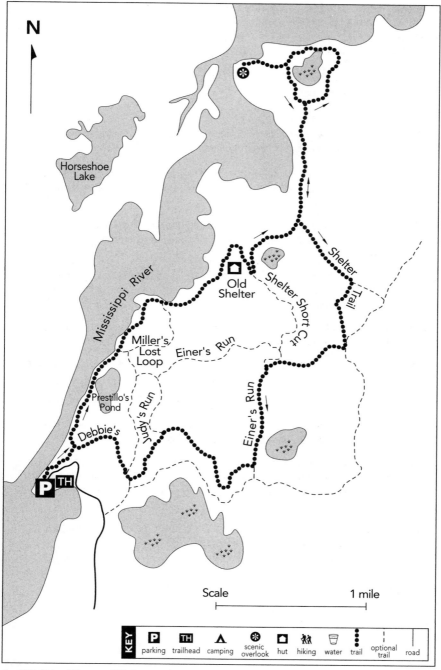

Jay Cooke State Park
Carlton, MN   (218) 384-4610

Distance: 12 miles
Ride time: 2 hours

Trail: Loops on single-track & paved trail
Rating: Moderate

Access: Take interstate 35W to the Carlton exit. Travel 4 miles east on MN Highway 210. Look for park signs.

Jay Cooke lies south of Duluth in the beautiful St. Louis River Valley. The paved William Munger Trail is always busy, but venture into the backcountry along a delightful single-track for great views of the St. Louis River and little traffic. A Minnesota State Park sticker is required to enter.

0.0 mi.   Park in the first lot on Highway 210. Cross over 210 and go through the opening in the wood fence. This single-track trail has exposed roots and rocks and may be wet.

1.0 mi.   Turn right onto a grassy trail at jct. 26. You may think you are traveling along a river, but you are actually pedaling along the slate outcroppings of Forbay Lake.

2.3 mi.   Cross over the dam at the end of the lake. At jct. 13 the trail splits. Either path brings you to the William Munger Trail. Turn right and pedal 2.1 miles on the paved bike path.

4.5 mi.   Turn right onto the Triangle Trail (3.5 miles). The trail meanders through wild flowers and beautiful stands of birch.

5.2 mi.   Stay to the right at jct. 17. There is a cut off to the left that avoids the steep climbs and boggy areas in the back section.

6.2 mi.   Jct. 18. Follow the trail to the overlook of the beautiful St. Louis River Valley.

7.2 mi.   After relaxing at the overlook, head back to jct. 18. Turn right and follow the main trail for 1 mile back to the William Munger Trail.

8.2 mi.   Turn right on the paved trail for .6 miles to the Oak Trail. Turn right onto the single-track and follow it to the left through the meadow and into the woods. This loop is moderate riding. Several hiking paths will join the trail, but stay to the right.

10 mi.   Follow the paved trail to the west for 2.6 miles. Cross over the bridge and turn left at jct 26. Return on the single-track.

Jay Cooke State Park

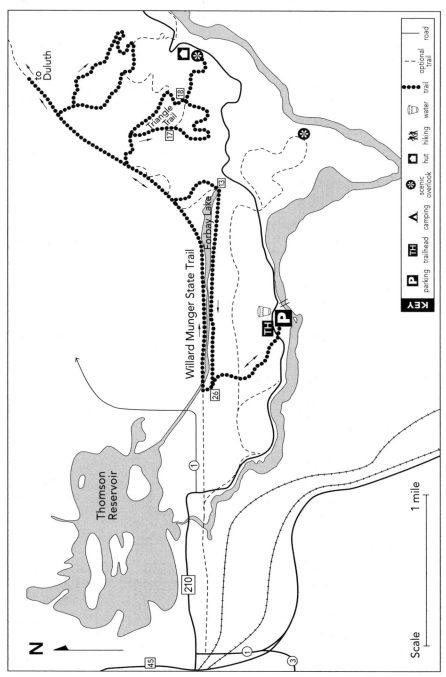

Paul Bunyan State Forest
Park Rapids, MN (218) 732-3330

Distance: 10 miles
Ride time: 1–1.5 hours

Trail: Single, two-track & forest roads
Rating: Moderate to Advanced

Access: Take MN State Highway 34 southwest from Walker, or northeast from Park Rapids to Ackley. From Ackley go 10 miles north on State Highway 64. Turn left onto Forest Road 2.

The Paul Bunyan State Forest supported red and white pines that were second to none in the region. Millions of board feet of virgin pine were cut here in the early 1900's. The logging lasted only 20 years, bringing with it a sort of boom and bust to the local communities. Many of the forest roads are actually old logging railroad beds. The forest lies on a glacial landscape called a "central ridge," a terminal moraine that sports many small ponds and bogs.

0.0 mi.   There is no parking and no marked trails. Park off to the side of the forest road after the powerline. Look for a small trail heading into the woods on your left. Pedal on a wonderful single-track. The narrow trail joins the main forest road. Turn left on the road and ride .2 miles.

0.7 mi.   Turn right onto the narrow trail. The many miles of single-track are virtually unmapped and used by local hunters. Feel free to explore any of the trails, but make sure to remember how to get back!

1.2 mi.   Take the dirt road marked Wildlife Area, to the left. Pedal through the clearing and look for a small trail cut into a young stand of aspen. Most of the conifers were wiped out in the early 1900's due to logging and successive fires which led to today's growth of aspen and hickory.

1.8 mi.   The trail pops out at another clearing. Cross the clearing and pick up the trail on the other side. Cruise down the hill on a small two-track and look for the single-track to the right.

2.1 mi.   The single-track continues on the other side of the road. Pick your way through rocks, roots and stumps.

2.6 mi.   Pass twin ponds to the right. The single-track becomes less rough. The small ponds and bogs that dot this area are depressions caused by small chunks of ice left from retreating glaciers 10,000 years ago.

3.0 mi.   There is a small marshy area to the left. Climb a challenging, rocky hill to a third clearcut area.

3.6 mi.   Turn right on the two-track. Pedal .6 miles to another two-track and veer left. This old forest road passes several trails. The map shows only the suggested route.

4.8 mi.   The two-track ends at a camp area. Veer left up the hill on a single-track. Three steep climbs and several technical descents make this an advanced ride.

5.6 mi.　The trail becomes wider at the top of a ridge. Near the middle of the descent you will see another single-track heading up the ridge to the left. Stay on the wide trail and follow it down the hill to the forest road. Take a right onto the forest road. Pedal 4 miles. At the "T" turn right and pedal .5 miles back to your vehicle.

Paul Bunyan State Forest

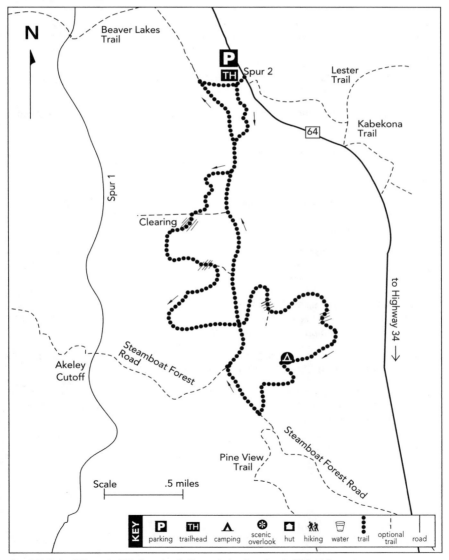

Pillsbury State Forest
Brainerd, MN (218) 828-2565

Distance: 10 miles
Ride time: 2 - 2.5 hours

Trail: Narrow snowmobile trails
Rating: Moderate to Advanced

Access: From Brainerd, MN go northwest on County Road 77. Turn southwest on Pillager Forest Road for two miles. Park on the east side of the road at the first trailhead.

The Pillsbury State Forest has 27 miles of wonderful rolling trails. The forest was heavily logged in the 1800's. Most of the logs were carried by sleigh or railroad to Gull Lake and then floated down the Gull River. In 1903 the first forest-tree nursery was established in the Pillsbury Forest.

0.0 mi.   The trail starts to the north of the restrooms. Expect several sandy pockets as you ride over Dahlstrom Ridge. The ridge is flanked by Prister Pond.

1.3 mi.   Ride up to the Little Devil's Ravine overlook. Then pick your way down a steep rocky hill.

1.6 mi.   Continue toward Sylvan Lake to the left. Look for interpretive signs to aid in tree identification. Another steep and rocky descent brings you along a small pond.

3.5 mi.   This is the turn-off to Sylvan Lake (1 mile one-way). Ride the old logging road under the hardwood forest canopy. These roads were built by hand in the 1880's. Cruise down the ridge and pass between two ponds.

4.6 mi.   Cross an earthen bridge. Pedal through the thick woods. The large boulders that seem out of place were carried into the region and dropped by an ancient ice sheet.

5.5 mi.   Where the trail splits, follow the orange marker to the right. You will cross this trail twice. Pedal past the John Meier homestead area. Ride around the end of Snag Lake and past Burned Camp Lake.

6.8 mi.   For those who have not had enough, continue on the trail across the road. Steep, three-tier climbs and similar descents lie ahead.

8.2 mi.   Turn left at the first intersection past Lost Lake. Finish with an easy ride back to the gravel road. Go south on the forest road to the trailhead. For a side trip, pedal 2.2 miles to the right up Pillsbury Peak.

Pillbury State Forest

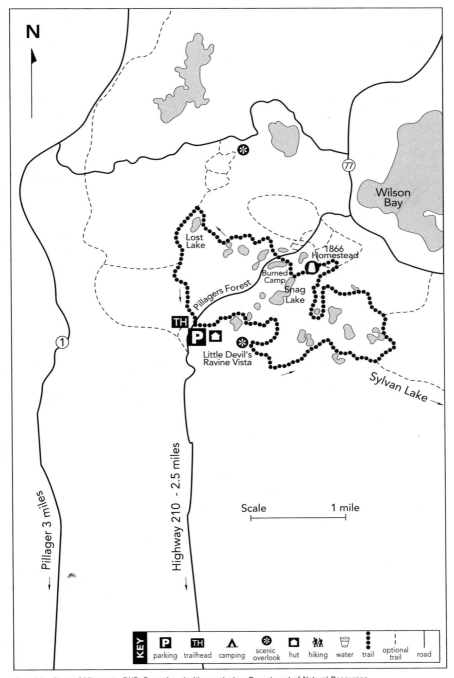

Savanna Portage State Park
McGregor, MN   (218) 426-3271

Distance: 6 miles

Ride time: 1 hour

Trail: Loop; grass trail, dirt road, single-track

Rating: Easy

Access: Savanna Portage State Park is located 50 miles west of Duluth and 135 miles north of the Twin Cities. Take Hwy. 65 north. Turn right at County Road 14 and follow it 10 miles to the park. A Minnesota State Park pass is required to enter.

Thousands of wooded acres make up Savanna Portage State Park. The park is named after the historical Savanna Portage which was a vital fur trading link between the St. Louis and Mississippi Rivers. There is good birdwatching, fishing, swimming and backcountry camping. All amenities are available.

0.0 mi.   Park at the boat launch. Find the trail closest to the lakeshore marked Shumway Lake Trail. The 2 mile loop around Lake Shumway is a smooth, gently undulating trail. The trail ends at the campground near site #20.

2.0 mi.   Find the trail near site #9. Follow this rolling trail for 1.6 miles. Stay to the right until you come to a gravel road.

3.6 mi.   Turn left and follow the road to the ranger station. At the "T", take a right. Find the first trail to the left. Ride along the ridge above the West Savanna Portage River.

4.2 mi.   Drop down to the Savanna Portage historical marker. This is a great place to hop off your bike and go for a short hike to the West Savanna River. Back on the bike, follow the dirt road a short distance past a parking lot. Turn right onto the snowmobile trail. This trail parallels the historic Savanna Portage for 1 mile.

5.2 mi.   Pedal through jct. G on the snowmobile trail.

5.6 mi.   At jct. 10 take the trail to the right and ride .3 miles to an unmarked intersection. Veer left to go back to the boat launch parking area.

There are 61 miles of snowmobile trails available for additional exploring. Check at the ranger station for a winter trail map.

Savanna Portage State Park

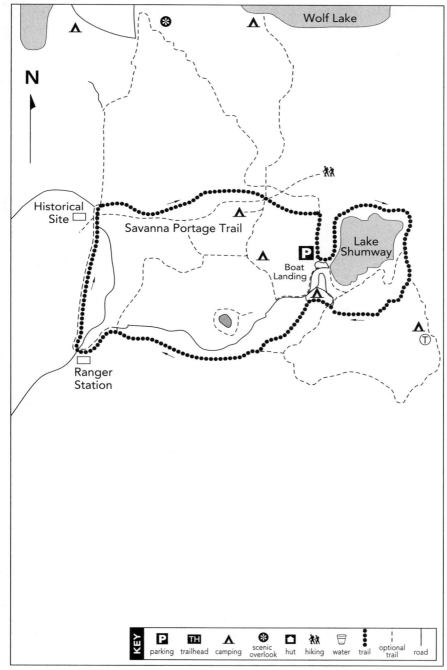

N

Wolf Lake

Historical
Site

Savanna Portage Trail

Lake
Shumway

P

Boat
Landing

Ranger
Station

KEY	P	TH	▲	✳	◻	🏃	🪣	⁝	optional trail	road
	parking	trailhead	camping	scenic overlook	hut	hiking	water	trail		

Simpson Creek
Deer River, MN

Distance: 10.5 miles (13 total) **Trail:** Single-track
Ride time: 1-1.5 hours **Rating:** Moderate

Access: The Simpson Creek trail is located 17 miles northwest of Deer River on State Hwy 48. Park at the DNR information center.

This rarely cycled trail is nearly all single-track. The gently rolling terrain takes the rider through red and white pines, along marshes, and up glacial eskers. Bring your fishing pole for some of the best walleye fishing around.

0.0 mi.   Park at the Cutfoot Sioux Visitor Center. Pedal on a paved trail a short distance and look for a narrow single-track to the right. Pedal under towering pines for a cool summer ride.

0.3 mi.   Cross over a dirt road FR 2190 and into a small cleared area

0.4 mi.   The trail splits and you can ride either way, but the most travelled trail will be to the left. The trails will rejoin at 1.1 miles. The open areas are perfect for berries and sun-hungry wildflowers.

1.4 mi.   After munching on wild raspberries along the trail you will come to a "Y", stay to the right.

1.6 mi.   At jct. "U" turn right for the outside loop.

1.9 mi.   You can stay on this trail and come out to Co. Rd. 33 or you can cut across to jct. "S" by taking the trail left.

2.2 mi.   At jct. "S" take the right hand trail and pop out onto Co. Rd. 33. Pedal to the left for .8 miles. Cross over the Simpson Creek. Keep a lookout for bald eagles and osprey who frequent this area from spring through fall.

3.1 mi.   FR 3245 turn left back into the woods. This will be jct. "A".

3.8 mi.   The trail will come to a FR road. Hop on the dirt road to the left and pedal .2 miles and turn left onto trail signed FR 3241.

4.3 mi.   At jct. "D" there will be a large three-way intersection, stay right for the outside loop. Pedal through jct. "E" and "F". Stay to the right through jct. "J". The trail will be a little overgrown and a bit rough at jct. "K".

6.0 mi.   Jct. "K" will loop around through an open area. and you will see a snowmobile trail on your right. Pedal left towards jct. "J". take the outside trail to Jct. "I".

7.5 mi.   Come to a large open three-way intersection among a stand of Red Pines, (jct. I). Stay right.

8.0 mi.   At jct. "M" take a right and cruise down the smooth hill. Cross over a small footbridge. Be careful-this little section has been known to cause big biffs. The wet and rooty trail is the most technical area you'll find in Simpson Creek

8.4 mi.   At jct. "T" take a right and pedal through an unmarked intersection, past jct. "N" and backtrack on familiar trail towards the parking lot.

Simpson Creek

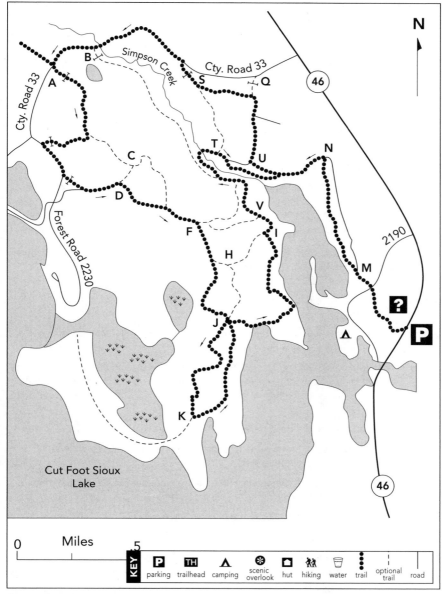

Spider Lake Trail
Backus, MN   (218) 947-3232

Distance: 8 miles
Ride time: 1.5 hours

Trail: Single-track, ski trails
Rating: Moderate

Access: From Pine River head west for 11 miles on County Hwy 2. Look for the Spider Lake trail on the south side of Hwy 2.

The Spider Lake trail is part of the Foothills State Forest in central Cass County. These trails aren't marked for mountain biking which means it is more rugged, more prone to change and more isolated. That means more fun, for some folks.

0.0 mi.   Park at the trailhead and pedal south.

0.1 mi.   At the four-way intersection turn right onto the black diamond ski trails. Look for moose in the marshy areas.

1.2 mi.   At the Y stay left and cruise up into the shady red pines, then out into a clearing for a pretty autumn view.

1.5 mi.   Cross an old logging road. This route can be used as a shortcut back to the trailhead. Grunt up the double decker hill. If you are looking for a less intense climb take the alternate trail to the left.

1.8 mi.   The trail splits. For the outside loop go right.

2.0 mi.   At the four-way intersection turn left. There will be a shelter on your right and a nice view of the lake. Go forward for an easy pedal down the logging road, or for the longer trail, pedal left around the lake.

2.6 mi.   Fly down the rocky trail. There is a hairpin turn at the bottom. Stay left for the ski trails. The snowmobile trails go right.

2.9 mi.   Cross over the four-way intersection. The trail Y's, go right. Don't continue around the lake—it's a dead end.

3.4 mi.   The path splits, but meets back together a little further up the trail. This can be a confusing intersection; stay left and look for blue signs. There will be a big hill, but it looks worse than it is. For the weak at heart, there is an easier trail to the right.

3.9 mi.   Turn left stay on ski trails Miles of ATV trails intersect the ski trails.

4.1 mi.   At the intersection stay right and grunt up a short, rocky, steep hill and roll down to join the trail at the lake.

4.7 mi.   Come to a steep hill. Be careful; there is a big pot hole at the bottom which acts as a launching pad.

5.0 mi.   Cross the main forest road at the four-way intersection.

5.3 mi.   At the four-way go straight. There are several steep hills.

6.5 mi.   Continue on the main trail through a very mucky area.

7.0 mi.   At the "Y" the right goes out to the paved road. To the left goes up into the woods and down a hill. Turn right at the four-way jct. and pedal back to the parking lot.

Spider Lake Trail

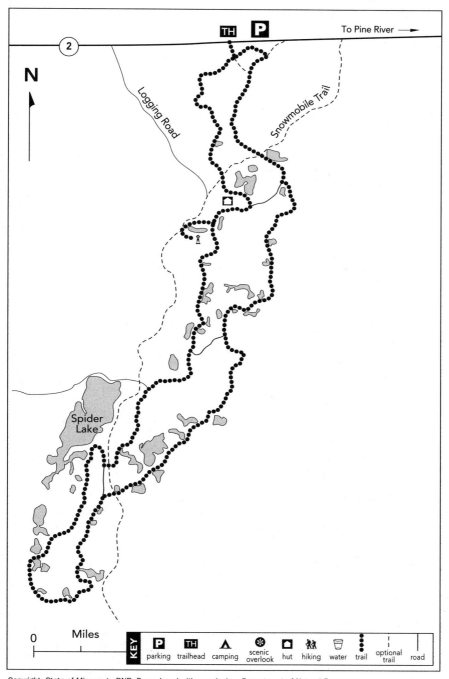

St. Croix State Forest
Danbury, WI   (218) 485-4474

Distance: 18 miles
Ride time: 3 hours

Trail: Loop on ATV trail
Rating: Moderate

Access: St. Croix State Forest is 22 miles east of Hinckley, MN on Highway 48.

Established in 1933, the St. Croix State Forest encompasses 44,558 acres. The terrain of the forest varies from gently rolling uplands to steep valleys along the St. Croix and Lower Tamarack Rivers.

0.0 mi.   Park at the Gandy Dancer trailhead in Danbury, WI. Ride north on the "rails to trails" trail. Cross over the St. Croix River. The flat gravel trail was our least favorite part of the ride.

2.5 mi.   Turn left and pedal through the woods a short distance. You emerge onto a dirt road. Follow the road .2 miles and turn right into the woods onto the ATV trail. The first part of the trail is fairly rocky, but flat. Stay with it, it gets better!

3.5 mi.   BE CAUTIOUS!! The downhill is very steep, sandy and rocky. Turn to the right on the road. Pass a gravel pile on the left and enter the trail on the right side of the road. The trail is very rocky, but ridable, and becomes more rolling as you approach the river.

6.7 mi.   Stay on the trail left of the Marksville Trailhead sign. The trail becomes fast and furious where ATV's have packed it.

8.5 mi.   Stay on the trail to the left and continue along the river. The next 3 miles are less rocky with many rolling hills. For a side trip, you can slide down the steep, rocky trail to cross the Tamarack River. There is a great backcountry campsite on the opposite side of the stream.

11.6 mi.   There is a scenic overlook of the St. Croix River at the edge of the small ridge. The trail becomes more rocky during the last 2 miles of the loop.

14.0 mi.   Follow the trail until it comes out at the gravel pile and the dirt road. Turn right and pedal up the road for half a mile.

14.5 mi.   Take a left at the sand pile and climb the steep, sandy and rocky hill. It is a challenge for even the advanced rider. At the top, get back on your bike and pedal the half mile to the dirt road. Turn left and pedal down to the gate.

15.0 mi.   Enter the trail around the gate. Ride .5 miles back to the Gandy Dancer Trail. Turn right and suffer through the 2.5 miles of deep gravel back to the trailhead in Danbury.

St. Croix State Forest

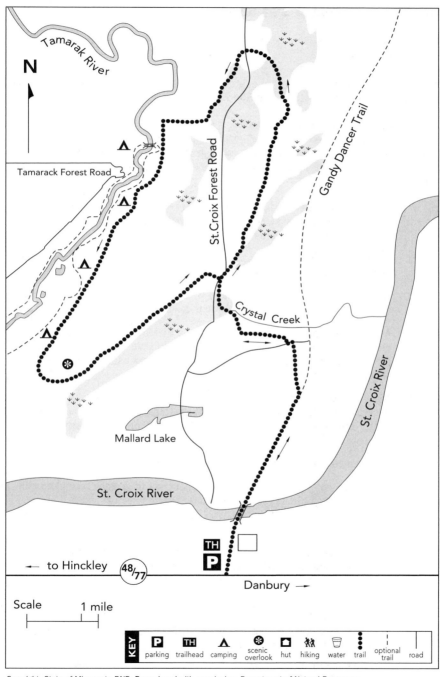

St. Croix State Park
Hinckley, MN   (612) 384-6591

Distance: 19.5 miles   **Trail:** Out and back on grassy two-track
Ride time: 3-4 hours   **Rating:** Easy to Moderate

Access: St. Croix State Park is located 15 miles east of Hinckley, MN on State Highway 48. Turn south on County Road 22.

This is Minnesota's largest state park, containing 33,000 acres of mature forest, meadows and marshes. The park is bordered by the beautiful St. Croix River which is a designated National Wild and Scenic River. All amenities are available. Our suggested route only includes half of the available mileage open to mountain biking. We do not include the 10 miles of gravel road west of County Road 22.

0.0 mi.   Park at the Trail Center. Turn left at the first large intersection east of the trailhead . The gradual slopes and granular soils are remnants of the glaciers that retreated from this area 10,000 years ago.

1.0 mi.   Climb a short hill. It may be sandy so keep to the edge. A trail merges from the right at .25 miles. Keep a lookout for wildlife.

2.3 mi.   The "Munger" trail continues to the right while a small footpath splits to the left. The sparse underbrush allows you to look deep into the forest.

3.2 mi   Another trail joins from the right. Stay on the trail to the left. Pass several new growth areas. The St. Croix has an abundance of white-tailed deer. The conifers provide shelter while the aspen is good browse. Black bears, coyotes, red and gray fox are among other wildlife that inhabit the park.

4.1 mi.   The tamaracks and black spruce bog you will be riding by is a great place for bird-watching. Much of the wetlands in Minnesota and Wisconsin are called "pit bogs;" depressed areas that were formed when a block of ice broke off the retreating glacier and was left behind to melt.

5.1 mi.   Enter a meadow. In the fall the tall grass is a deep red.

5.5 mi.   Turn left at the "T." This is a nice open spot great for a picnic, complete with rustic outhouses. Cross over Wilbur Brook Creek on a small bridge. The trail becomes more rolling. Climb up a small hill and turn right at the top. (The left trail is foot traffic only.)

6.8 mi.   The best is saved for last. The trail rolls up and down over smooth terrain through a mixed hardwood forest of oak, aspen, maples and pines. Ignore several unmaintained trails, they have a tendency to dead-end.

9.5 mi.   A gate indicates the park boundary. Pedal past the gate and out of the park. A short steep climb brings you near the end of the trail. Parallel an old logging road and pedal an additional mile to County Road 48. Retrace the trail back to the trailhead for a total distance of 19.5 miles.

(For more adventure or increased mileage the Munger trail continues on the other side of the road.)

St. Croix State Park

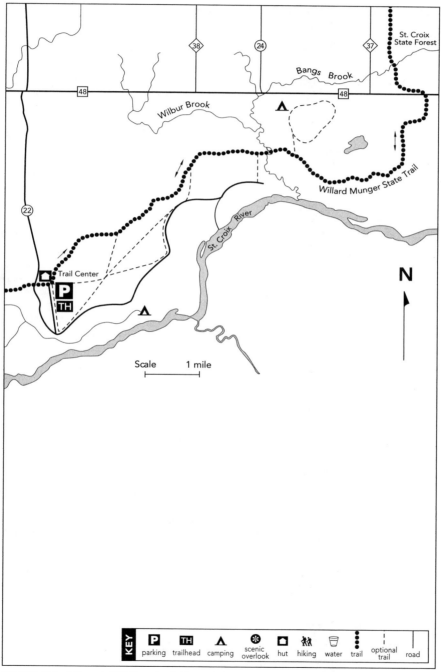

Sugar Hills Trail
Grand Rapids, MN   (800) 472-6366

Distance: 12 miles   **Trail:** Rolling hard-packed ski trails
Ride time: 3 hours   **Rating:** Moderate to Advanced

Access: From Grand Rapids, MN drive 7 miles south on Highway 169. Head west on County Road 17, (Sugar Lake Road), following the signs to the parking lot.

The Sugar Hills trail system is a great roller-coaster ride, with its many peaks, valleys and ridges. A climb up Big Thunder Peak gives you a sweeping view over a dense forest of sugar maples with numerous spring fed streams and lakes. The trail frequently follows old logging roads that were built by hand in the 1800's. This little used trail is a delight for the mountain biking enthusiast. At the start of our ride a pileated woodpecker stopped 30 feet away on a dead aspen and proceeded to hunt for breakfast.

0.0 mi.   Take the trail farthest to the right of the hut. Stay to the right at the bottom of the hill. New trails have been cut, so make sure you keep a sense of direction.

0.2 mi.   Turn right at jct. G for the outside loop. The trail here is less traveled with low areas that may be wet. Climb a hill to jct. F

1.3 mi.   Continue uphill and to the right. (The route left takes you to the trailhead.) Climb a very steep hill. Here the unmowed trail joins the main trail. Pedal across a rustic plank bridge, then up onto a small ridge, flanked on the left by Long Lake. Descend a steep hill to a three-way intersection. This is jct. E, veer right.

2.3 mi   An unmarked trail joins from the right. There are many miles of these unmarked, outback trails that you might want to explore.

2.4 mi.   Climb a steep, technically challenging hill. The trail splits in .3 miles. Stay to the left. The trail rolls through a beautiful mixed forest that is home for a diverse range of wildlife.

3.3 mi.   Turn left at jct. C, a three-way intersection. Climb several hills and fly down the other side. Pedal another mile to the next junction.

4.2 mi.   A spur trail merges from the right. At jct. D take a right.

4.4 mi.   Keep right at the next intersection. The south side of the trail system can be very confusing. Many unmarked trail intersections make it a challenge to keep to the main trail.

4.6 mi.   Half way down the hill there is a "T", take a right and climb to the top out of a bowl. At the top of the hill turn right.

4.9 mi.   At the bottom of the hill turn left for the outside loop. Pedal up the grassy area paralleling the ski hill.

Continued on page 88

Sugar Hills Trail

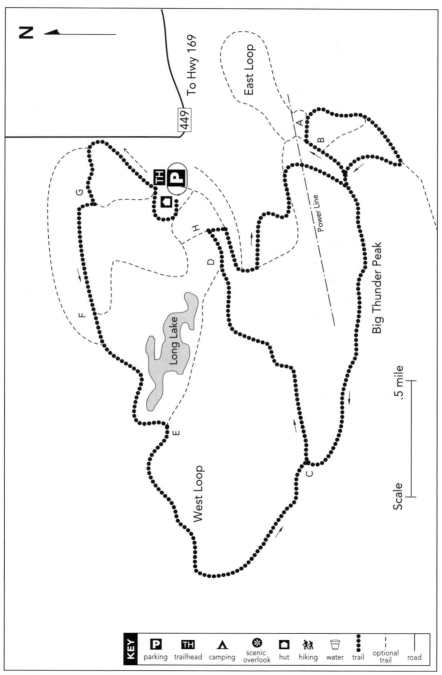

USGS 7.5 Series, Reproduced with permission.

5.4 mi.   Parts of the ski trail are wet and unridable. Climb the ski hill on the maintenance road. Cross a utility road under a powerline and climb nearly 1 mile to the top of Big Thunder Peak. The long climb is worth the view. This area is named for its abundance of sugar maples and is incredibly beautiful in the fall!

6.5 mi.   Directly to your left is a "no snowmobiles" sign. Take the trail immediately to the left downhill. Pass jct. B and jct. A.

7.0 mi.   The trail "Y's." Go left back to Big Thunder Peak. This back loop has short, steep climbs and technical descents. (The trail to the right will take you back to jct. B.)

8.4 mi.   The trail splits; the junction has arrows pointing right and left. Turn right and climb the hill. At the top, turn left. You are now on the trail back to Big Thunder Peak. At the top the trail joins the road.

9.4 mi.   Ignore a small trail splitting off to the right.

10.2 mi. Ride downhill and veer right at jct. C. Turn right at jct D and head back to the trailhead for a 12 mile ride.

You might want to take food and water with you. Many miles of unmarked trails make it easy to get lost.

Honey, will this be covered by homeowners or auto?

Suomi Hills
Grand Rapids, MN   (800) 472-6366

Distance: 21 miles
Ride time: 3 hours

Trail: Varied trail surface from grassy to rocky ski trails.
Rating: Moderate to Advanced

Access: 14 miles North of Grand Rapids, MN on State Highway 38. There are two parking areas to these trails. We used the southern lot. There are toilets, but no water.

The Suomi Hills areas is a wonderful ski area in the winter and is an underused mountain biker's haven in the summer. The area has a variety of terrain from grassy and rolling to rough and rocky. However, there are plenty of loops that allow you to pick your poison.

0.0 mi.   Pedal up the dirt road a short distance and around a gate onto the trail. Roll up and down the trail as you cruise through stands of birch and aspen.

0.5 mi.   Pass through the first intersection and take the Big Horn Trail to the right through the birch and maples.

1.8 mi.   Roll down and across a small earthen bridge. Climb a short, steep hill to a signed, three-way intersection and continue straight ahead. A few boggy areas can make this slow going.

2.6 mi.   The grassy trail passes a remote campsite and then crosses a worn footpath that leads down to Orange Lake.

2.9 mi.   On the other side of FR. (2153) the trail is smoother and dryer.

3.9 mi.   Pass a rustic lakeside campsite on Kramer Lake.

4.5 mi.   Come to a three-way jct. Follow the trail to the right (blue arrow). If you want a workout, fly down the hill, but beware of a hairpin turn at the bottom. Climb a long steep hill; at the top turn right for the toughest section of the trail. Pedal along the ridge above Pot Hole Lake.

6.5 mi.   Ride next to Spruce Lake. Look for a "ranger box" to your right and a secluded campsite to your left. Look across to the island and see if you can spot another campsite. Note the wild irises, morning glories and raspberries.

6.6 mi.   At the Y take the left trail. The right hand path is a canoe portage.

7.4 mi.   Plunk yourself down on a bench for a great view.

8.0 mi.   Don't miss the caution sign for a "big downhill."

8.3 mi.   At the T turn right. A trail will join from the left, which is Beaver Lake Trail and can be very wet.

8.9 mi.   The trail comes out to a dirt road. Turn left to the parking lot, then ride around the gate and back onto the trail. Ride along a small pine plantation on your right.

Continued on page 92

Suomi Hills

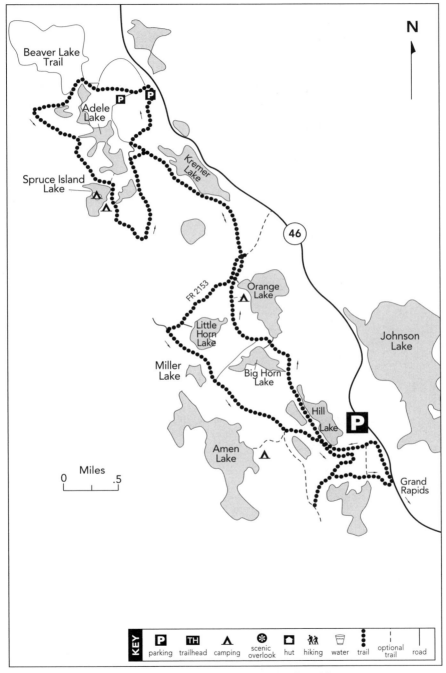

9.7 mi.   At the familiar jct. take an immediate left and climb a long hill.

11.4 mi.   Pedal back to FR. (2153). For the adventurous person, take the dirt road to the right. Cruise past Little Horn Lake.

12.4 mi.   Look for a little used path on the left towards Miller Lake. This tight single track will wind close to a boggy area.

12.8 mi.   Pull up a bench and catch the scenery of Horn Lake.

13.1 mi.   At the Y stay to the left. The trail to the right is a foot path to Miller Lake.

13.3 mi.   Climb a short steep hill and at the top stay to the right.

14.0 mi.   Several short climbs later will bring you to a three-way intersection. Stay left for the parking lot.

Wow, "The North Country Guide To Mountain Biking" said veer left?

Washburn Lake Trail
Outing, MN   (218) 947-3232

Distance: 13 miles
Ride time: 1-3 hours

Trail: Two loops on grassy/dirt trail
Rating: Easy to Moderate

Access: From the Twin Cities take 169 north to Garrison. Take Highway 6 north to Outing. Go west on County Road 48, half a mile. Keep your eyes open; brush has overgrown the trailhead sign. Park on the north side of County Road 48.

The Washburn Lake Recreation Area is 2,500 acres of wilderness with 26 miles of trails in six different loops. The Washburn Lake Trail lies mostly in the Land O' Lakes State Forest where the rolling trail is dotted with lakes and small ponds. There are outhouses, but bring water.

0.0 mi.	The North Loop starts in the northeast corner of the lot. The trail is easy, but not flat.
0.4 mi.	At the "T", follow the trail to the left. Soon the trail splits again. Veer left and ride down the hill near Washburn Lake. This smooth, grassy trail is an ideal loop for a casual ride. It is especially nice on a cool morning or a fall day.
1.8 mi.	Leave the lake through nearly pure stands of maples. Ride .25 miles to where the trail splits. Stay left. A few washed-out areas make the trail a little tricky for a novice.
2.4 mi.	Turn left for the suggested route. Descend to a small, pristine lake. Grunt up two short hills through a young stand of quaking aspen.
4.2 mi.	Turn left for the last leg of the first loop.

SOUTH LOOP

0.0 mi.	Cross County Road 48. Ride to the right along Grasshopper Lake. Climb the ridge for a nice overlook. Then head under the powerline and across a dirt road.
0.6 mi.	Veer right where the trail "Y's." Notice that the south loop has more stands of oaks then the north side. Look for several huge white pines that survived the devastating logging era between 1880-1890.
1.0 mi.	At the 5-way intersection cross the gravel snowmobile trail onto a grassy trail. There is a low area here. Crisp air, beautiful colors and a thin shell of ice showing on the lake make this a wonderful fall ride.
1.2 mi.	Cross a snowmobile trail. Turn left where the trail splits, (not under the powerline).
1.8 mi.	The trail splits again. Take the trail to the right up a ridge above the lake.
2.4 mi.	Cross a dirt road and jog left. Turn right onto the grassy trail. A black diamond trail joins from the left. Stay on the main trail, riding on a ridge flanked by several ponds.
4.4 mi.	A rustic shelter is found 2 miles from the end of the trail. Pedal a short distance to where the trail splits. Turn right to stay on this suggested loop. (The left trail skirts Bear Lake.)
6.0mi.	A small trail merges from the right. Continue to the left and climb a short hill. The trail forks at Bear Lake. Turn right onto the rolling trail which parallels a dirt road. Turn left onto the trail marked "no motorized vehicles." This trail leads you back along Grasshopper Lake and across the paved road to the parking lot.

Washburn Lake Trail

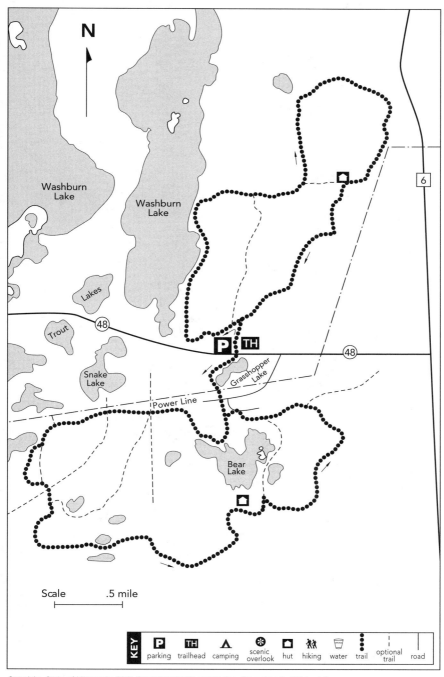

N

Washburn
Lake

Washburn
Lake

Lakes

Trout

48

Snake
Lake

Grasshopper
Lake

48

6

Power Line

Bear
Lake

Scale   .5 mile

KEY | P parking | TH trailhead | A camping | ✳ scenic overlook | ⬜ hut | 🚶 hiking | 🥤 water | ⋮ trail | ┊ optional trail | │ road

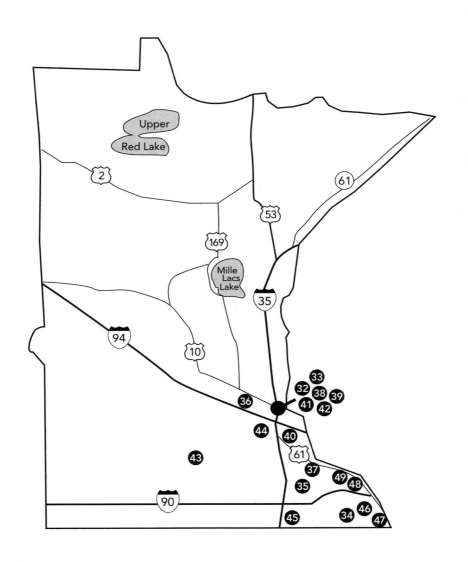

The North Country Guide to

Mountain Biking

SECTION 3

Metro/Southern Minnesota

32   Afton Alps

33   Battle Creek

34   Brightsdale Unit - R. Dorer State Forest

35   Bronk Unit - R. Dorer State Forest

36   Elm Creek Park Reserve

37   Kruger Unit - R. Dorer State Forest

38   Lake Elmo Park Reserve

39   Lawrence Unit - MN River Valley State Park

40   Lebanon Hills

41   Louisville Swamp - MN River Valley State Park

42   Mounds Springs - MN River Bottoms

43   Mount Kato Mountain Bike Park

44   Murphy-Hanrehan Park Reserve

45   Myre - Big Island State Park

46   Oakridge/Wet Bark Trail - R. Dorer State Forest

47   Reno Unit

48   Snake Creek Trail - R. Dorer State Forest

49   Trout Valley Trail - R. Dorer State Forest

Afton Alps Mountain Bike Park
Hastings, MN   (612) 436-1320

Distance: 5.5 miles
Ride time: .5 - 1 hour

Trail: Open grassy and wooded single-track
Rating: Moderate

Access: From St. Paul, east on Hwy. 94 to the County Rd. 95 exit (Stillwater exit). Go south on 95 through Afton. Turn into the Afton State Park complex. Do not go right into the State Park facility but turn left and go to the golf/mountain bike clubhouse.

Afton Alps is following a current summer trend; turn a downhill ski area into a mountain bike park. The trails have been cut across the ski hills and utilize most of the wooded sections between the ski runs to create some good technical single-track sections. A trail pass is required.

Leaving the clubhouse look for the start of the trail on the north side. Cruise down the Afton loop adjacent to a ski run. Climb up the switch backs of Deep Woods Express. You will be treated to some impressive views for your efforts. Fly down Afton Gully and Last Chance Gulch, but not <u>too</u> fast or you might get launched into the woods.

At the bottom of the gulch turn onto Deer Path trail. Work your way up to the Hideaway trail for a great view of the St. Croix River Valley. It's a colorful treat in the fall. Continue riding along the bottom of the ski runs on Cruising Meadow trail past the meadow chalet. Begin a gradual climb, but make sure to turn onto the Bridge trail for one of the best sections of the park. You will be working up to Cliffs Edge and Southern Switch backs as you finish this 5.5 mile loop.

CONTROL YOUR BiCYCLe!

IMBA Rules of the Trail

Afton Alps Mountain Bike Park

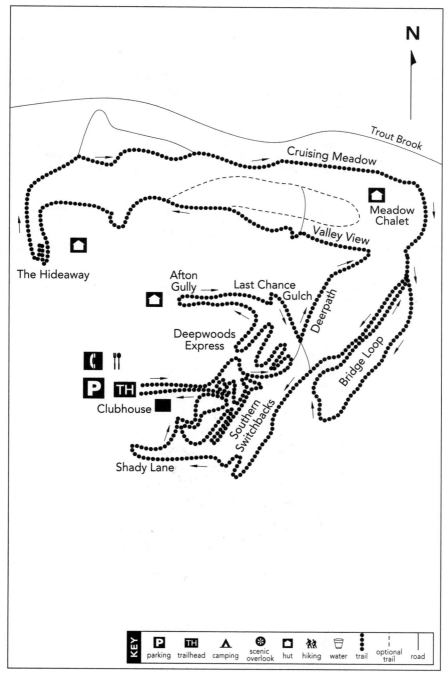

Reprinted with permission from Afton Alps Mountain Bike Park

Battle Creek
Ramsey County, St. Paul   (612) 777-1707

Distance: 5 Miles
Ride time: 1 hour

Trail: Cross country ski trails/hiking trails
Rating: Moderate to Difficult

Access: From South St. Paul at 494 take Hwy. 61 north. Exit on Lower Afton Road turning east. Continue east to Winthrop Street about 1/2 mile to parking area on left hand side of the street. Facilities are not available.

Battle Creek is a city park that has been host to both mountain bike and cyclocross races. This biking playground offers varied terrain with single-track sections that branch off the ski trails. These tough sections test brakes, bike skills and climbing prowess. If you want to keep the ride moderate keep to the ski trails that wind through open fields and into hardwood forests.

It's unlikely that this park will ever have an up-to-date map; at least one that shows all the intertwining single-track. We suggest you show up and be ready to explore. You can't get lost. It's simple, If you encounter any city streets you have gone out of bounds, go directly to jail, do not pass go! But, just backtrack to where you came from and explore some more.

A reminder: City parks are multi-use and you will likely encounter walkers on the wider trail sections; this is their park, you are a guest, be nice!

NeveR SPooK ANiMALS!

IMBA Rules of the Trail

Battle Creek

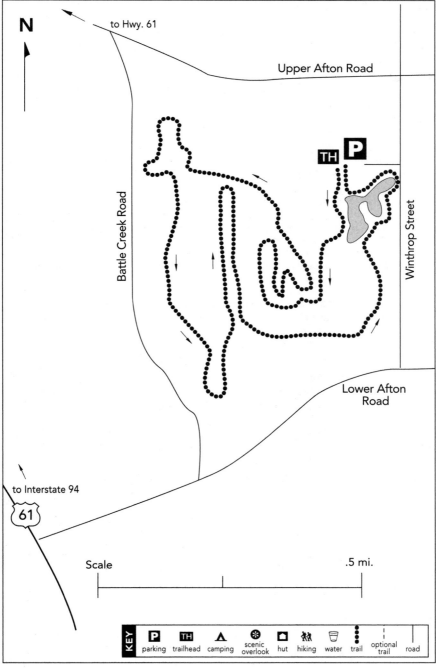

Reprinted with permission from Ramsey County Parks and Recreation Department

Brightsdale Unit
Preston, MN   (507) 765-2740

Distance: 5 miles   **Trail:** Grassy ski trail
Ride time: 1 hour   **Rating:** Easy to Moderate

Access: From Lanesboro, MN take State Highway 250 north 2 miles. Take the dirt road west for 2 miles. Park at the Forest Resource Center where restrooms and water are available.

Brightsdale Forest Unit lies in the beautiful Lanesboro Valley only 2 miles from the popular Root River State Trail. The non-profit Forest Resource Center conducts forest research and offers instruction on mushroom hunting and building bat condos as well as a course called "Ropes in the Sky." Historic Lanesboro offers winetasting, Amish shops and wonderful bed and breakfasts.

0.0 mi.   Pedal south away from the Forest Resource Center through the yard. There is an overview of the Root River to your left. The cliff is steep so be careful. From the overview, coast nearly half a mile downhill to the river valley.

0.8 mi.   Turn left at the bottom of the hill. Pedal through a plantation of white pines. Ride .1 miles and stay right. This is an easy ride so enjoy the sounds of the songbirds.

1.5 mi.   The trail crosses the dirt road and heads up a gradual hill under a canopy of maples. Pedal into a plantation of white pines, cross over a small creek bed, and traverse the opposite side of the small valley to an open field.

2.3 mi.   Stay to the left and climb the hill at the three-way intersection.

2.5 mi.   Cross over a gravel road into the woods. The trail becomes well-packed in the shade of the dense forest. In the fall the trail is buried under crispy fallen leaves of oak and hickory trees that dominate the river bluffs.

2.8 mi.   Stay to the left at the "Y." Go downhill and cross a small gravel road. The trail comes out at the base of the Resource Center. Pedal .2 miles, cross a small driveway, and turn right onto the grassy trail.

3.5 mi.   Heading downhill along an old creek bed notice that a trail joins from the left: This is the long descent that started the route.

4.3 mi.   Stay right and climb out of the valley. Turn left where the trail splits at the top. Ride for .3 miles and take the trail to the right.

4.9 mi.   The trail crosses the road and heads back into the woods. At the bottom of the valley veer right. End the ride at the base of the Resource Center.

Brightsdale Unit

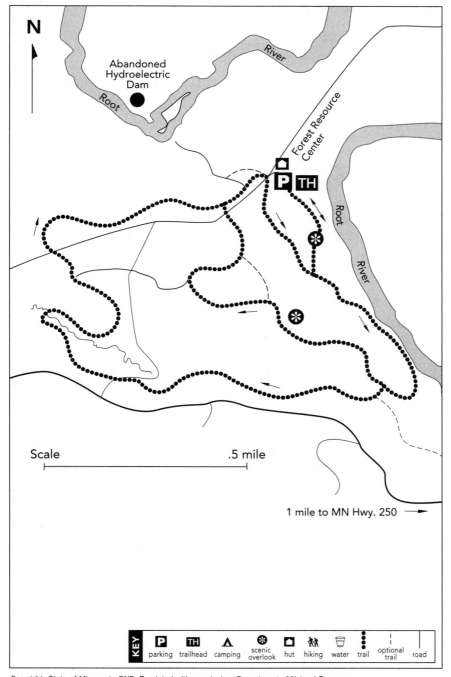

Bronk Unit
Wabasha, MN   (507) 523-2183

Distance: 7.7 miles   **Trail:** Wide hard-packed ski trails
Ride time: 1-1.5 hours   **Rating:** Moderate

Access: From Winona, MN take Highway 61 northwest to US Highway 14. Turn left on County Road 14. Go north on County Road 23. Turn right onto Township Road 6. Watch carefully for this road, it looks like a driveway. Travel east on 6 for half a mile to the trailhead.

The Bronk Unit situated 500' above the surrounding valleys, straddles the ridge between the Mississippi River Valley and Stockton Valley and provides beautiful scenic overlooks of the oak and hickory covered slopes. These are the only marked mountain biking trails in the Richard J. Dorer State Forest.

0.0 mi.   Park at the lower lot. Pedal around the gate and climb .6 miles on a dirt road to a 4-way intersection at the top of the hill. Take the gravel road to the left around the gate. Notice the trail goes in either direction. Take the trail to the left.

1.8 mi.   Turn left and ride the gravel road for a short distance. Be careful not to fall over the edge trying to take in the beautiful views of the valleys on either side.

3.8 mi.   Turn left and follow the trail to an overlook of the Stockton Valley. This is a great place for a break and a picnic. On the trail again, a road merges from the right.

5.0 mi.   Cross over a foot path that goes down to a rock outcropping. Pedal .75 miles to an overlook of the Mississippi River Valley. Hop off your bike and walk out on the point.

5.6 mi.   Another overlook is to the left. Bring your binoculars on this ride and check out the variety of birds that migrate up the Mississippi River corridor in the spring and fall. When the bald eagles are migrating you can spot hundreds of birds at one time. Check with the MN birders' hotline for migration information.

6.0 mi.   Turn left at the next intersection onto a small dirt road. Pedal .2 miles and veer left for the last leg of the loop.

6.8 mi.   Pop out onto the dirt road and ride to the left. Ride .6 miles down the dirt road. There are dips built into the dirt road, these spots are great for catching air!

Bronk Unit

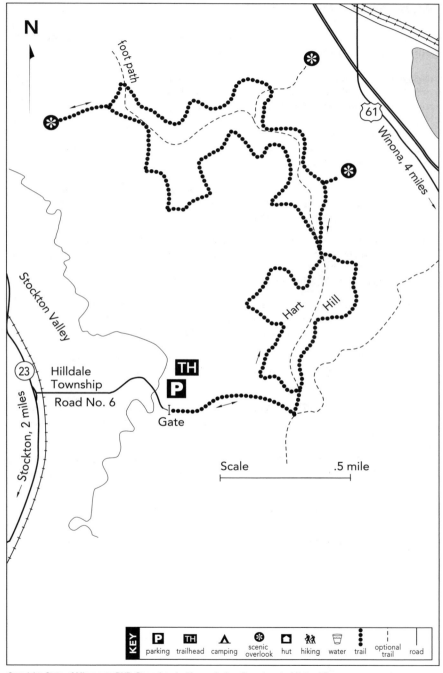

Elm Creek Park Reserve
Maple Grove, MN   (612) 424-5511

Distance: 5 miles   **Trail:** ski trails, short sections of paved trail
Ride time: .5 - 1 hour   **Rating:** Easy

Access: From Minneapolis take I-94 west to 694 west. At County Road 81 go north 5.5 miles. Watch for the Elm Creek Park Reserve sign on the right. You will need a Hennepin County Park sticker to enter the park.

Elm Creek is one of the few parks in the metro area that actually allows and encourages mountain biking. The loop is generally flat, but toss in a little mud and several short climbs and it becomes a great first-time, fat-tire experience.

0.0 mi.   Park at the Visitors Center. The trail starts on the service road to the right of the building. Hang a quick right onto the trail and head downhill. Be careful, there is a sharp turn at the bottom.

0.3 mi.   Ride along the tall bushes and cattails. Cross over the marsh on a boardwalk. Watch out for the geese!! Continue to ride along the marsh for .3 miles. Where the trail splits, climb the short hill to the right for a nice view of Mud Lake. Look for the blue herons that like to hang out here.

2.0 mi.   Cross a dirt service road and climb the steepest of several short hills. If it is wet this hill can be a challenge! Turn left onto the paved path. Pedal a short distance to pick up Meadow Trail on the right.

2.6 mi.   The bumpy Meadow Trail pops out onto the paved path long enough to find the trail to the right. This trail may not be marked for bicycling but it is part of the mountain biking trail system.

2.9 mi.   Turn right and pedal .75 miles on the paved road around the swimming beach. Cross Pavilion Road. The little lake is a great place for a dip on a hot, muddy day!

3.7 mi.   Near the top of a short incline stay to the left where there is an unmarked trail. At the "Y" veer left. (The path to the right is well worn, but is a walking path to the beach.)

4.2 mi.   Turn right onto the paved path where the mountain bike trail ends.

Hennepin County Parks Trail Hotline: (612)559-6778

Elm Creek Park Reserve

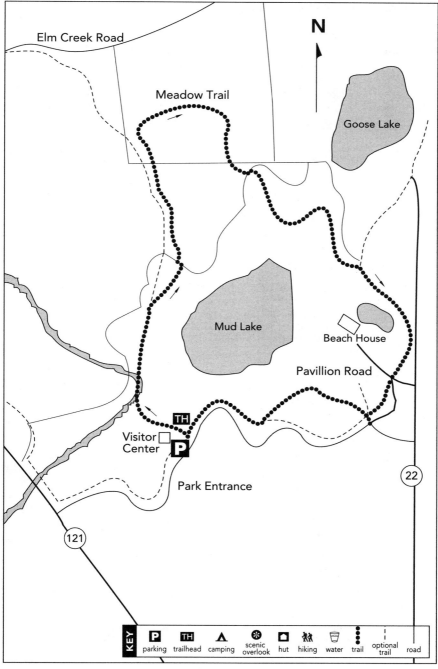

Hennepin Parks, Reproduced with permission.

Kruger Unit
Wabasha, MN (612) 345-3216

Distance: 6 miles (8.5 total)
Ride time: 1-1.5 hours

Trail: Double-track; small section of single-track
Rating: Moderate to Advanced

Access: From Wabasha, MN go west on State Highway 60. Go south on County Highway 81. Drive past the campground. Take the next entrance on the left (2.5 miles) on a small dirt road past the ranger station.

Kruger, like much of Richard Dorer State Forest, is made up of great limestone bluffs that overlook sprawling valleys. The steep slopes are covered with walnut, oak, maples and cherry. The rugged trails in the Kruger Unit climb the bluffs and traverse the valley of the Zumbro River.

0.0 mi.   Take the trail out of the parking area and into the woods. Pedal through the first three intersections staying to the right.

0.3 mi.   Go right where the trail splits. Follow the path up the hill marked with orange arrows. Stay to the left at the top. Large stands of mature oaks, ash and hickory make this an ideal habitat for a variety of wildlife.

0.7 mi.   Cross several dry creek beds. (Depending on the time of year these may or may not be dry.) Cross the last sandy creek bed, take a hard right, and attempt the steep hill. Once at the top pedal along the opposite ridge.

1.2 mi.   Turn right into the woods and climb .7 miles. Do not be surprised if you flush out a flock of wild turkeys.

1.9 mi.   Turn left at the top of the bluff and pedal on a flat trail for half a mile. This limestone bluff supports mostly grassland with scattered norway pines, sumac and an occasional apple tree–a tasty fall snack.

2.4 mi.   Stay to the right where the trail "Y's". Pedal .1 miles. At the second "Y" go left .5 miles to an overlook of the picturesque Zumbro River Valley.

3.5 mi.   Take a left and go downhill at the familiar intersection. Be careful! There may be rocky, washed-out sections. The climb out of the valley is extremely challenging.

4.1 mi.   Pedal past the campground and turn left onto the single-track. The trail widens as it turns uphill for .5 miles. This is a technical climb with loose, rocky soil and a steep pitch.

4.8 mi.   Pop out at the top, catch your breath, and take a right to another overlook. As you come back from the overlook, take the small spur trail to the right.

5.3 mi.   This trail is very steep and technical with erosion control timbers placed across the path.

5.8 mi.   At the bottom you are on the wide trail where you started. Take a right and pedal a short distance back to the trailhead.

Kruger Unit

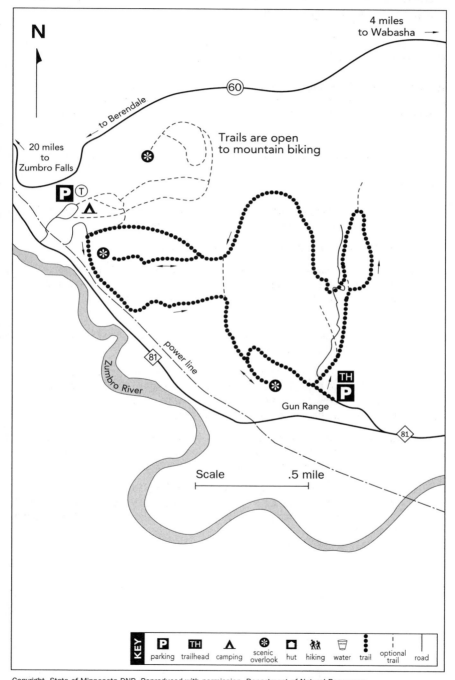

Lake Elmo Park Reserve
Lake Elmo, MN   (612) 731-3851

Distance: 8 miles
Ride Time: 1 hour

Trail: Grassy two-track
Rating: Easy to intermediate

Access: Lake Elmo is located east of St. Paul off I-94. Head north on County Road 13 to Hwy. 10 east. Follow the signs to Lake Elmo Park Reserve. A parking fee is required. All amenities can be found at the park information center.

Lake Elmo has designated 8 miles of it's 20 mile trail system for mountain bike use. The gently rolling terrain is shared with hikers and horses. This rolling terrain provides a moderate ride for a family outing.

0.0 mi.   The trailhead is at the north end of the parking lot. Pedal onto the trail going to the left. Pass jct. 19 and roll casually along the edge of the lake.

1.0 mi.   Stay to the right at jct. 17 on the smooth two-track.

2.0 mi.   At jct. 30 you can choose the trail next to the lake and pedal under the oak trees. Or choose the outside prairie trail for a little longer ride. Pop out at the top of a small hill where the outside trail joins from the left. This is marked jct. 29.

3.0 mi.   Pedal a short distance to jct. 28. Take a left for the outside loop and climb a short hill; the trail rolls along hugging the woods.

4.0 mi.   Climb a small hill up to a three-way intersection (jct 26.) Turn right and pedal a short distance to jct. 25; take a right and cruise down the only good-sized hill. Be careful. A few ruts and rocks make this section a little more technical. Pedal through the prairie along the edge of the park.

5.0 mi.   Cross over a farm road and continue along the edge of a field, climb a short steep hill and turn right. Follow the gravel road to the equestrian center. Ride through the campground following the road around to the left.

6.0 mi.   Take a right at the three-way intersection and ride along a series of ponds. At jct. 22 stay left near the edge of woods. Ride through jct. B and turn left at jct. 21. At jct 14 take a right and cruise on the hard-packed, rolling trail back to the parking lot.

Lake Elmo Park Reserve

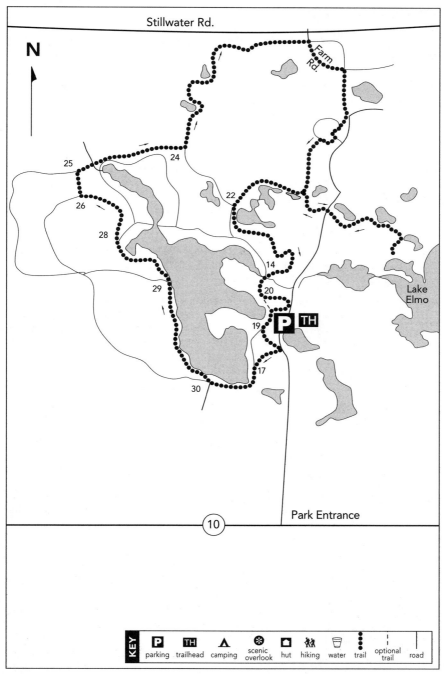

Reprinted with permission from Washington County Park

Lawrence Unit - MN Valley State Park
Jordan, MN   (612) 492-6400

Distance: 6.1 miles   **Trail:** Loop on snowmobile/ski trails
Ride time: 1-1.5 hours   **Rating:** Easy

Access: Located between Jordan and Belle Plaine. At the stop lights on Hwy. 169 go north on Co. Rd. 9 for .25 miles. Turn left on Co. Rd. 57 (look for park sign with the wood duck). Park trail center is located approximately four miles down Co. Rd. 57.

The Minnesota River Valley was carved out by the Glacial River Warren. At the close of the Ice Age a broad valley and much smaller, meandering Minnesota River was left behind. This state park has a rich historic heritage with the Dakota Indians. The Lawrence Unit includes the only remaining building from the 1850's town of St. Lawrence. There is a shelter at the trailhead with running water and toilets. Also available in the park are camping facilities. A Minnesota State Park sticker is required for the Lawrence Unit.

0.0 mi.   North of the trail center, ride past the gate and take the snowmobile trail to the left. You will start in an open prairie and quickly enter the forest along the river banks. Notice Beason Lake to the south.

0.5 mi.   Just after Beason Lake there is a connector trail that provides access to the ski trail. This could be an important option if the snowmobile trail is wet and muddy. This trail provides many opportunities to see the Minnesota River. You may also have an opportunity to view muskrats, mink, beavers or raccoons in the wetlands. The gigantic cottonwoods, silver maple and basswood trees lining the edge of the river are flood tolerant and historically have escaped natural fires.

2.5 mi.   At the "Y", follow the trail to the right up a gentle slope. Leave the river bottoms and return to the open prairie. Ride .2 miles up to the only remaining building from the 1850's town of St. Lawrence.

2.7 mi.   Leave the building site and ride back down the same trail you just came up on. Stop at the first intersection.

2.8 mi.   Veer left and ride on the grassy prairie trail to the west.

3.4 mi.   Take a left at this "T" intersection. In a short distance cross over County Road 57. The topography changes from prairie, to rolling oak savanna uplands. There are several wooden plank bridges over the marshy areas. You will ride behind the park information center. Maps, information and toilets are available.

4.3 mi.   Proceed straight ahead, passing the trail to your right. Look for white tail deer and red and grey fox in the uplands. Red-tail hawks are also plentiful feeding on rodents.

5.7 mi.   Cross over Co. Rd. 57 and ride the last .4 miles back to the trail center. Make sure you stop at the information center on Co. Rd. 57. There you will be able to pick up detailed maps that show many more miles of trails that are open to mountain biking. The staff supports mountain biking as a sport. Give them your thanks.

Lawrence Unit - MN Valley State Park

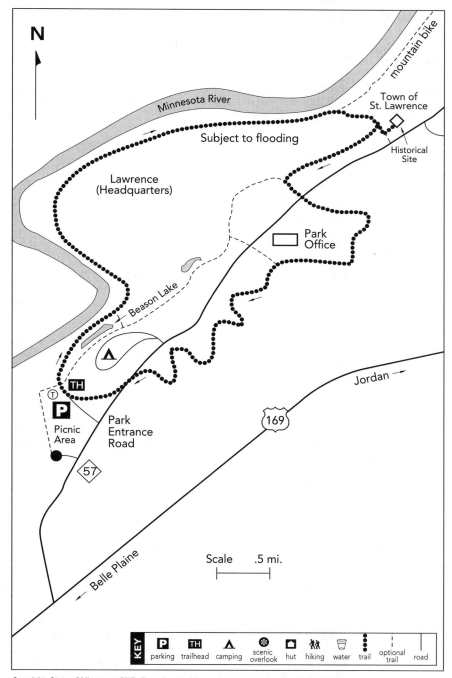

Lebanon Hills
Eagan, MN (612) 437-6608

Distance: 2.5 miles & 1.4 miles
Ride Time: 30 minutes

Trail: Loop: dirt ski trails
Rating: Moderate

Access: 35E south to Cliff Road. East on Cliff Rd. to Johnny Cake Ridge Road. It is about .25 miles to the parking lot on the west side of the road. Water is not available at the trailhead.

Lebanon Hills is a short but challenging mountain bike trail. Located in dense hardwoods, this trail provides a hilly challenge to even the expert mountain biker.

Long Loop:

0.0 mi. Just past the gate veer right and begin a gradual climb up a dirt double-track trail. Ride across the hiking trail. DO NOT ride on the hiking trail!

0.2 mi. This is the short loop cutoff. We suggest you ride the long loop first and ride the short loop on your second lap to add some variety.

0.7 mi. At the next hiking trail intersection stop and hike up to your right for a great view of the Minneapolis skyline. Return to your bike and ride on the biking trail down a slight hill. Cross another hiking trail and then an exit to Galaxie Ave. on your right.

0.9 mi. Cross another hiking trail. You will encounter a couple of granny gear climbs up through heavily wooded forests. Be careful of potentially fast, rocky descents off these hills.

1.5 mi. This is the intersection where the short loop joins the long loop from the left. Be cautious here; right after this intersection you cross another hiking trail. This is a downhill section with several banked turns. You will notice a trail coming in from your right, a short distance after the downhill section. This is an unmarked foot trail that goes out to Johnny Cake Ridge Road. Continue straight ahead.

2.3 mi. Just before the trailhead the trail splits. Go left to finish the long loop. Riding straight ahead will bring you to the parking lot.

Short Loop:

0.0 mi. Ride back up the gradual climb and past the hiking trail intersection.

0.2 mi. Turn left, riding through a grassy open area.

0.3 mi. Cross over the hiking trail, and proceed straight ahead.

0.5 mi. This is a "T" intersection with the long loop coming in from your right. Be cautious at this intersection. Riders from the long loop will be going fast and have the right of way! Turn left and be prepared for downhills with banked turns.0.6 mi. Cross over the hiking trail and pedal straight ahead. Ignore the foot trail on your right, and finish the short loop at the parking lot. These loops can be repeated to add more miles for an after work ride.

Lebanon Hills

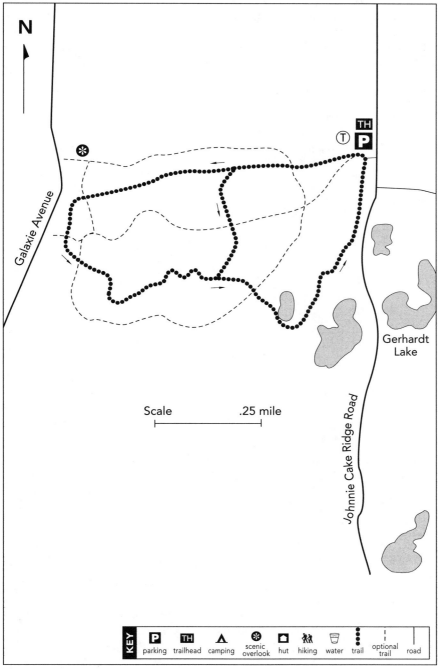

Dakota County Parks, Reproduced with permission.

Louisville Swamp - MN Valley State Park

Jordan, MN   (612) 492-6400

Distance: 6.6 Miles   **Trail:** Loop on grass and dirt ski trail
Ride time: 1-1.5 Hours   **Rating:** Easy to Moderate

Access: Located 4 miles south of Shakopee, MN. From Highway 169 take
145th Street north. Look for a State Park sign. Follow 145th Street
approximately .5 miles to the trailhead.

The Dakota Indians inhabited the Louisville Swamp area up until the mid 1800's. During the 1850's settlers living in this region changed the face of the land with their farming practices. Consequently, Louisville Swamp now floods three years out of five. You should check with park managers to determine the condition of the trails. B.Y.O.B "Bring your own binoculars" as this wetlands attracts thousands of songbirds during annual migrations through the valley. Outhouses are available but not running water.

0.0 mi.   The trail begins just beyond the information board. Immediately after riding on crushed limestone you will encounter the Little Prairie Trail. Continue straight ahead on the Mazomani Trail. Ride this trail southwest on the edge of a prairie to a bluff overlooking Louisville Swamp. Follow this bluff and traverse a moderate downhill.

0.4 mi.   Follow the trail left. Stop to see the Ehmiller homestead. Ride into the bottomland forest where a bridge crosses Sand Creek to a forested island.

1.2 mi.   Veer right and cross over another bridge. You will now exit the bottomland forest.

1.5 mi.   A gravel road continues straight. Follow Mazomani Trail to the right. A "house-size" boulder dropped by a glacier during a recent glaciation invites you to test your climbing skills. Follow the bluff edge through oak savannas.

2.5 mi.   The Jabs farm is a great place to envision life as it was in the 1800's. Ride south away from the swamp.

2.8 mi.   Follow the Carver Rapids loop by veering right. Ride through more oak savannas. The land managers are working to restore the natural prairie land by annual controlled burns. During the fall you will have a couple views through the trees of the Minnesota River.

3.7 mi.   Turn left and climb this bluff, heading back towards the Jabs Farm.

4.2 mi.   Notice the beginning of the Carver loop on your left. Continue straight ahead. Watch for wildlife such as fox, deer, and many species of songbirds.

4.5 mi.   Ride past the Jabs farm and cross the creek over a boulder causeway placed here after the floods of 1993.

5.0 mi.   After climbing the hill follow the trail to the right for great panoramic views and an opportunity to observe various species of waterfowl. Did you remember your binoculars?

6.1 mi.   Turn right and grunt back up the hill towards the open prairie.

6.4 mi.   Ride past the Little Prairie Loop and back to the trailhead. All trails in this unit are open to mountain biking. You may want to take in some of the trails that run along the banks of the Minnesota River. You can get information on these trails from the map at the trailhead.

Louisville Swamp - MN Valley State Park

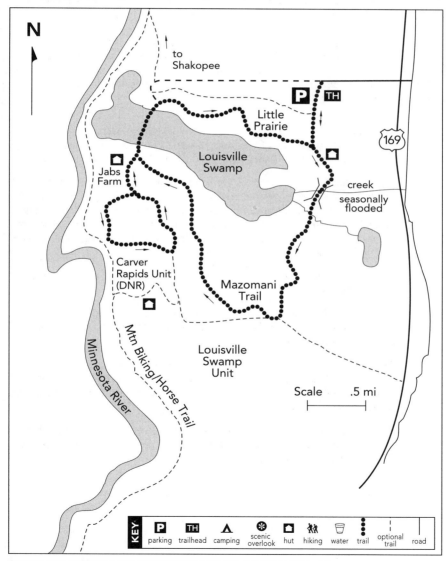

MN River Bottoms -
Mound Springs
Bloomington, MN   (612) 887-9601

Distance: 10 miles one way   **Trail:** Narrow, hard-packed trail
Ride time: 1-2 hours   **Rating:** Moderate

Access: From Minneapolis, MN drive south on Interstate 35W. Exit at 98th Street and head east to Columbus Avenue. South on Columbus Avenue one block, then left on 99th four blocks. Park at the Indian Mound School.

The Minnesota River Valley has a rich history of fur trading and trapping. The river valley was gouged out by Glacial River Warren, the outlet for the great glacial Lake Agassiz. The "Minnesota River Bottoms" is one of the most popular trail areas for metro mountain bikers. The official trail is 3.3 miles. There are, however, many additional miles that run along the river west of the 35W. Sections of the trail outside of Mounds Springs are susceptible to flooding.

0.0 mi.   Pedal south one block on 11th Aveune. The trail heads down into the woods where the city street turns to the west. Follow the trail downhill across several shallow drainage areas. During rainy years this can be deeply washed out.

0.6 mi.   Take a right at the intersection at the bottom of the hill. (The trail to the left heads into the wildlife preserve area and is off-limits to mountain bikes. Go for a hike and check out the unique flora and fauna and the worldclass birding that exists in the river valley.) Climb a steep hill. Timbers have been placed across the trail for increased footing while hiking. The trail is wide enough that you can ride on either side and avoid the timbers.

1.1 mi.   Cross a low spot that is normally wet and climb to the top of a hill. There is a small picnic area.

1.3 mi.   Turn left and ride down the other side of the hill. Follow the lowlands along the river bottoms. The path bends and turns with many trail spurs. It is easy to recognize the main trail.

2.6 mi.   Take the trail to the left down into the valley and along the edge of the river. The official ride ends before you cross under 35W. The trail flattens out and continues all the way to the Bloomington Ferry Bridge. Retrace the trail back to Indian Mounds school.

The trail continues under 35W. However, there is a section of backwater that is crossable only in dry seasons. The flood of 1997 has left large sand deposits on some of the trails west of 35W.

MN River Bottoms - Mound Springs

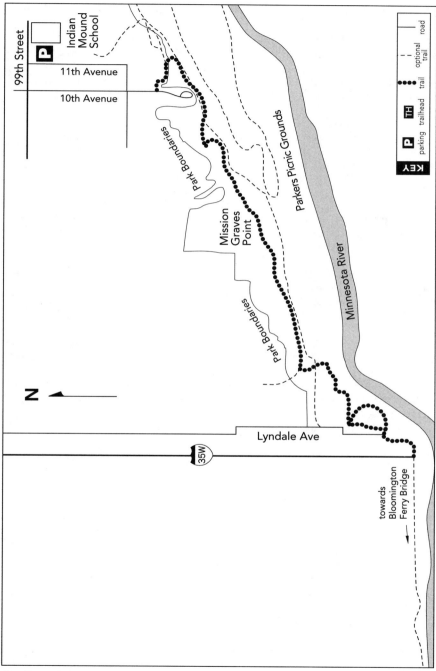

City of Bloomington map.

Mount Kato Mountain Bike Park
Mankato, MN (800) 668-5286 (507) 625-3353

Distance: 7 miles
Ride time: 1-1.5 hours

Trail: 90% single-track
Rating: Beginner to Advanced trails

Access: From Mankato take Hwy. 169 south to Hwy. 66. Drive 1 mile south and follow signs to the Mount Kato Ski & Bike complex.

Mount Kato Mountain Bike Park opened in the summer of '96. A trail pass is required and can also be used at Afton Alps Mountain Bike park. Bike and helmet rental is available. The highlight of Mount Kato's mountain biking is the beautiful yet challenging Main Loop. This loop includes some beginner sections, but is mainly an intermediate ride. The Main Loop has three climbs, three descents and is 4.5 miles in length.

To begin the Main Loop, start at the base of the ski area and climb up the Kato Climb (the beginner ski hill). This tends to be a very good warm-up, with its ten switchbacks and about 200 vertical feet of climbing. Once it starts to level out you loop around Frog Pond and then across to Overlook Traverse.

The Overlook Traverse goes along the top of the ski area and climbs another 40 vertical feet to the top. This is just one of the incredible views the area has to offer. From the Traverse trail go over Snow Pond bridge and loop around Back Bowl pond then into the woods.

Once in the woods you will descend Gets Tight trail which has a hairpin turn and a narrow exit, then over to Cedar Climb. From the top of Cedar Climb go around a pond to the trail called Killer Toad Loop and over the top of another great downhill called Low Line. The next climb is called Staircase. After Staircase you will ride past Lookout, Snow Pond and on to Compressor. This decent has seven switchbacks and winds down through some very big oaks. Once at the bottom take Cabin Run back to the front of the ski area and across the base of the mountain.

First timers may want to stop and take a break, while those who want more adventure can try off-shoots to the main loop called Pink Poodle, Dead Horse and Quick Release. Have fun and ride safely.

Mount Kato Mountain Bike Park

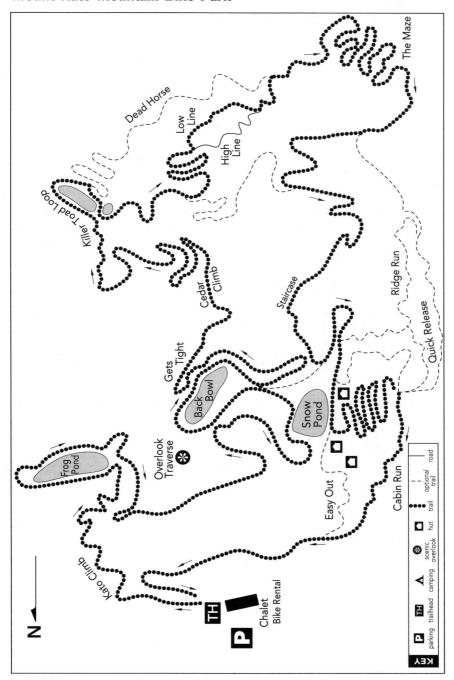

Murphy-Hanrehan Park Reserve
Prior Lake, MN   (612) 447-6913

Distance: 6 miles   **Trail:** Loop on hilly ski trails
Ride time: 1-1.5 hours   **Rating:** Moderate to Advanced

Access: From Minneapolis, MN take I-35W south. Go west on County Road 42. Turn left on Hanrehan Lake Blvd. and left on County Road 75.

Murphy-Hanrehan is the best excuse to take your bike off-road for a great roller coaster ride. Murphy's terrain is ideal for mountain biking, but also subject to heavy erosion. The bike trail is open from August 15 to October 31st, from 5:00 a.m. to 10:00 p.m. daily. The trail system is carefully monitored and will be closed if conditions are too wet. Call ahead for trail status. There are outhouses but no water available at the trailhead.

0.0 mi.   Park at the trailhead and ride south on the far right hand trail. Pedal through a short section of meadow until you climb into a narrow, wooded corridor. Some areas will be single-track while most will be double-track. "Murphy" is one of only several nesting areas in Minnesota for the Hooded Warbler. The trails have been closed near this site. Stay on the designated bike trail.

0.8 mi.   Climb the hill and pedal through jct. 11 and 10.

1.5 mi.   The trail loop starts at jct. 9. Cruise down the hill, but be careful of a sharp turn at the bottom. This area has a tendency to be boggy.

1.8 mi.   Climb a long steep hill to jct. 7. At the top you can choose the kamikaze downhill to the right or the semi-kamikaze to the left. Pedal through beautiful, rolling, oak-covered hills.

2.7 mi.   Where the trail "Y's", bear to the left and go for a rollercoaster ride. Pass by a lake and a marsh on your right. Chances are there will be mud. Please do not venture off the designated trail. Trails with closed gates are not open to mountain biking.

4.3 mi.   The loop finishes at jct. 9. Take another turn around the loop by going to the left, or turn right onto the two-way trail back to the trailhead for a total distance of 6 miles.

Call before you ride!

Hennepin County Parks Trail Hotline: (612)559-6778

Murphy-Hanrehan Park Reserve

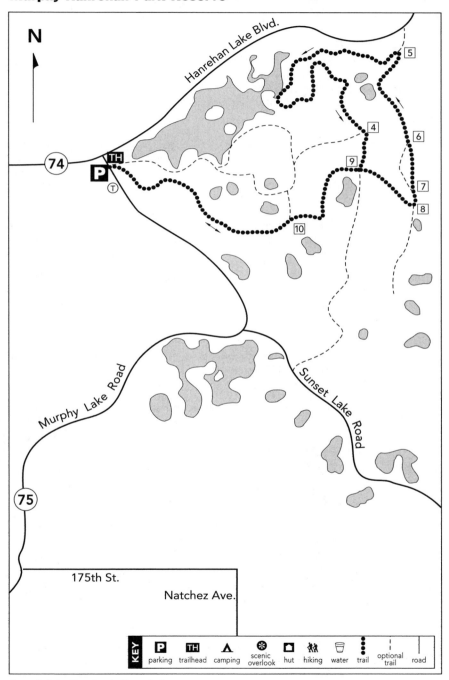

Hennepin Parks, Reproduced with permission.

Myre Big Island State Park
Albert Lea, MN   (507) 373-4492

Distance: 7 miles   **Trail:** Grassy hiking trails
Ride time: 1-1.5 hours   **Rating:** Easy

Access: Myre Big Island is located three miles southeast of Albert Lea, MN. Signs for the park can be seen from either I-90 or I-35. Take Exit 11 off I-35 and follow the park signs.

Driving through south central Minnesota one wonders where there could possibly be any mountain biking other than through the soybeans and corn. Gradually the landscape becomes more undulating as you approach Albert Lea. "Big Island" is situated within the Bemis Moraine, created 10,000 years ago when the last glaciers retreated northward leaving the park with gently rolling hills and lakes. All amenities are available at the ranger station.

0.0 mi.   Park behind the ranger station. The trail starts across the park road. Ride through the prairie around the edge of a small wetland. This is hawk country so keep your eyes open for birds surfing on the wind currents.

0.3 mi.   Turn left near the campground and left again into a small section of woods. Descend the hill for a view of Albert Lea Lake. Look for White Pelicans. They are becoming more common on area lakes, especially during fall migration. Pelicans are hard to miss with their 6-foot wing spans.

1.0 mi.   Take a right for a loop along the lake where the trail splits. Look for blue herons and wood ducks. The trail winds in and out of the trees as it follows the edge of the lake. You will pass several secluded, hike-in campsites on Albert Lea lake. Check on their availability with the ranger if wish to camp here.

2.0 mi.   The trail heads away from the lake and up onto a small ridge for a nice view of the lake and the island. Ride .6 miles and cross under the powerline. Cruise a short distance and veer to the right towards the Esker Trail. You can avoid the long climb ahead by taking the trail to the left where it parallels the esker.

3.1 mi.   Take the trail to the right. Ride high up on the narrow, snaking Esker Trail. This high vantage point is a good place for bird watching. Try to spot indigo buntings, song sparrows and red-wing black birds.

3.8 mi   Descend the Esker Trail through the oak savanna. The lower trail joins from the left before heading into the prairie. To the left, on the edge of the woods, is a rustic picnic shelter and a workinghand pump.

4.8 mi.   Turn right at the junction at the bottom of the hill and ride back to the park entrance. Add a loop by turning left at the campground. This loop is 2 miles long and returns on the other side of the campground.

Myre Big Island State Park

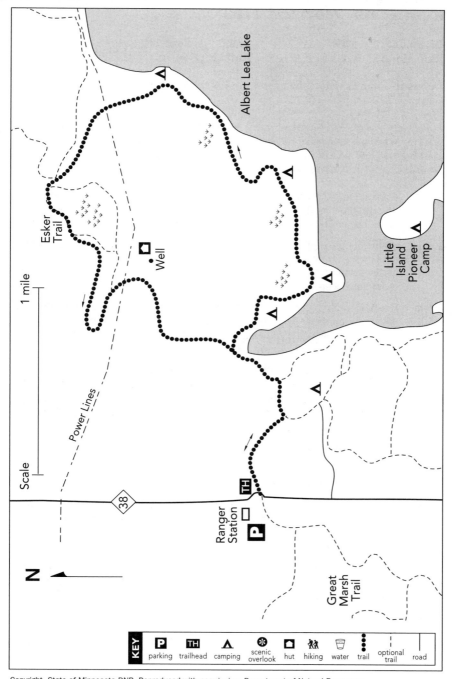

Oakridge/Wet Bark Trail
Houston, MN   (507) 523-2183

Distance: 8.6 miles   **Trail:** Hard-packed/grassy loop
Ride time: 1.5-2 hours   **Rating:** Easy to *Advanced

Access: From Houston, MN travel west 5 miles on County Road 13 to the Oakridge Trailhead.

The Oakridge Unit of the Richard Dorer State Forest is similar to other units with its steep oak and hickory covered slopes and grassy, hill-tops. Unlike the other units where you first ride up to the top of the bluff, this trail starts at the top. The fun drive up on the switchbacks reminds one of a more mountainous region. Outhouses and water are available at the trailhead.

0.0 mi.   Park at the trailhead. Pedal around the gate and onto the field road. Ride through the corn field .5 miles and take a left where the field ends and the trees begin. Cruise downhill until you come to your first intersection. Stay left.

1.6 mi.   At the bottom of the hill bear right at the field. Pedal across an earthen bridge and through a meadow. Duck into the cool shade of the woods and ride the valley bottom along a creek bed. The steep valley is a reminder that this region went untouched by the ancient glaciers.

2.8 mi.   The trail switchbacks to the left and starts to climb. A moderate incline turns into a narrow single-track ascending the valley wall. A sharp drop-off, coupled with a steep pitch and narrow trail, makes this a very tricky section. The trail becomes a little wider as you climb the last section of the hill.

3.8 mi.   At the top catch your breath and turn left for an overlook of the surrounding bluffs and valley. Ride away from the overlook. Pedal to the top of the hill and then along the edge of a farmer's field. After half a mile veer right near a small pond into the woods. Ruffed grouse and the elusive wild turkey thrive in this area and your chances of spotting both are excellent.

5.0 mi.   Stay left where the trail splits and climb the hill.

5.5 mi.   The trail "T's" at the top of the hill. Go right onto the field road. This is the start of the 2.3 mile long inside loop.

6.2 mi.   Turn into the woods to the right for the overlook. The Richard Doer State Forest is noted for its breathtaking views of the surrounding valleys. In the fall, you may want to spend a little extra time in the forest gathering walnuts, butternuts and hickory nuts.

Ride back from the overlook and onto the trail to the right. Follow the trail just on the edge of the forest. The open fields offer an opportunity to spot any soaring hawks or falcons. The inner loop merges with the outer loop. Climb the hill and turn right on the field road.

*A short section of technical single-track gives this ride an advanced rating.

Oakridge / Wet Bark Trail

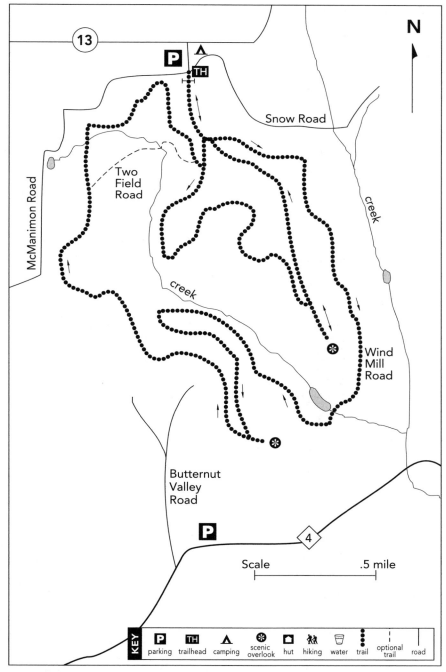

Reno Unit
LaCrescent, MN   (507) 724-5264

Distance: 10 miles
Ride Time: 2 hours

Trail: Narrow two-track, some dirt road
Rating: Advanced

Access: Take Hwy. 26 17 miles south of LaCrescent to the village of Reno. Go west through Reno. Follow the gravel road for 1/4 mile to parking area.

The Reno Unit is part of the Richard Dorer State Forest. This hardwood forest is made up of deep valleys and steep ridges that overlook the Mississippi river. This 13.3 mile trail system challenges you with a 500 foot rise in elevation and beautiful scenic vistas. There are five rustic campsites with water and outhouses at the trailhead.

0.0 mi.   Trailhead, parking area. Look for the trail by climbing up the small gravel road. The trail climbs the bluff and parallels the creekbed below. You will gain 350 feet in the first mile.

1.0 mi.   The trail levels out for a short distance, pedal along a white pine plantation.

1.2 mi.   Come to a three-way intersection. The trail straight ahead will take you to a backcountry campsite with nice views of the valley. Turn right for a hairy descent. You will find that most of this trail is either up or down and has lots of switchbacks.

1.6 mi.   Pass a foot trail on the left and climb .3 miles to another backcountry campsite. Here you will find a fire pit and pit toilets.

The trail becomes more moderate with less severe climbs and descents.

3.1 mi.   Fly down a steep hill and cross a dry creekbed. In the spring, count on splashing through this area.

3.3 mi.   Enter a short section of trail on private land. Be courteous.

4.0 mi.   Huff and puff up a long steep section; this will be a lung buster for even the advanced rider. The best part is at the top; the trail mellows out and you can catch a breather as you pedal along the ridge.

4.3 mi.   The mellow trail doesn't last for long. Can you say "Pebbles and BAM BAM?" The trail takes a wicked turn and plunges back down into the valley. The rocky, loose terrain means *hang on to your brakes*!

4.8 mi.   The trail follows alongside the creekbed for nearly 1 mile.

5.5 mi.   The trail will T. Turn right and gently climb through the mixed hardwood forest. Keep an eye open for wild turkey.

5.8 mi.   Pass through the gate and continue the gentle climbing; a trail will join from the left.

6.0 mi.   Finish your climb up to a narrow, gravel, field road. Turn right and pedal .2 miles. The gravel road T's, take a right onto a single-lane, country road and pedal past small farms for 2 miles. Look east towards the Mississippi River Basin. You will see a rock formation called Fairy Rock.

Gorgeous views! Here the road descends. Be careful-even the road has switchbacks.

9.0 mi. At the bottom of the hill, look on your right for an obscure single-track, and duck back into the woods. Pedal one mile along the river back to the trail head.

Reno Unit

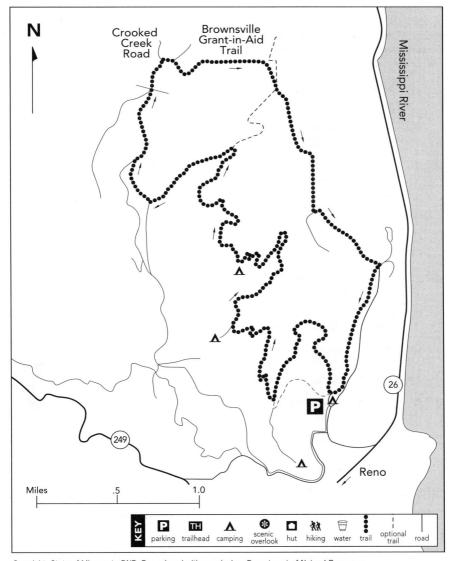

Snake Creek Trail
Wabasha, MN   (612) 345-3216

Distance: 10 miles
Ride time: 2-3 hours

Trail: Grass and hard-packed dirt trail
Rating: Moderate

Access: From Wabasha, MN take U.S. Highway 61 south. Signs for Snake Creek are seen on U.S. Highway 61 The access road doglegs to the right, but continue straight on the field road. Park where the road ends.

Snake Creek, named for the small trout stream that cuts through the unit, is like much of the Richard Dorer State Forest--rugged. The trail winds its way to the top of the 300' bluff through hardwood forests for a wonderful view. Climbs with reasonable grades and nice long descents make this an enjoyable ride.

0.0 mi. Ride around the gate and up the moderately steep field road.

0.2 mi. The trail will start to your right. Pedal on the trail through a planted field and across a low area. The trail seems to end, but look for orange markers in the woods to your left.

1.3 mi. The trail splits. Stay left and climb .5 miles up to Rattlesnake Ridge. Look over your shoulder for a nice view of the valley. This is a well-packed trail with no loose rocks.

1.8 mi. At the top of the bluff take the field road to the right for .1 miles. Veer right onto the snowmobile trail and climb up to another field road.

2.2 mi. Take the field road to the left. Pedal through open fields.

2.9 mi. Turn left onto the trail, where the field road turns right. The open bluff tops with an abundance of rodents and snakes make this good hawk country.

3.6 mi. Duck into the edge of the woods and ride along an old fence line. This section becomes fast as you start to descend. Cruise downhill for over .5 miles.

4.8 mi. The trail veers to the right at the bottom of the hill. The trail is washed out in spots so be careful here. Ride along Snake Creek as the trail traverses the ridge. Turn right at the junction with a private tree farm.

6.2 mi. The trail joins a dirt road. Climb .5 miles back to the top of the bluff. Turn left next to the fence and cruise up and down over gently rolling terrain.

7.9 mi. The trail "T's" at a field. Go right. Then turn left into the woods where the trail splits. Follow the trail down into the valley. Cross over an earthen dam and pedal to the next intersection.

8.7 mi. Turn left and backtrack through the field to the dirt road.

9.5 mi. At the dirt road take a left and head back .5 miles to the trailhead.

Snake Creek Trail

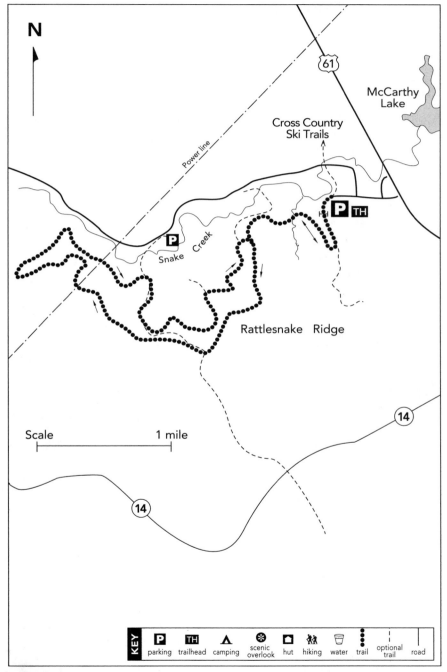

Trout Valley Trail
Wabasha, MN (507) 523-2183

Distance: 8.5 miles   **Trail:** Hard-packed dirt trail with rocky hills
Ride time: 2 hours   **Rating:** Easy to Moderate

Access: From Winona, MN take U.S. Highway 61 north to County Road 29. Follow County Road 29 west for 1.75 miles to the trailhead.

The Trout Valley trail, named for the trout creek that runs through this section of the forest, is a multi-use trail that connects the valley bottom with the wooded ridge and flat bluff-top. Panoramic views of the Mississippi River Valley, Whitewater Valley and the Trout Creek Valley are the highlight of this ride. There is no drinking water available.

0.0 mi.	Park at the trailhead. You are in for a stiff climb of nearly 300 feet in the first .7 mile.
0.3 mi.	The trail splits, stay to the right. Ride up the hill to the top of the bluff. The trail has loose rocks and a steep pitch.
0.6 mi.	The trail becomes less steep after a switchback to the left. This is a great place to catch your breath. Grunt up the last little bit of trail to the top of the bluff. Congratulations! You made it!
0.7 mi.	Take the trail to the left at the 4-way intersection and pedal along the edge of the clearing.
1.8 mi.	The view over Trout Creek Valley is stunning, especially in early October when the oak and aspen are in full color. Cruise through stands of red and white oak, and several plantations of white pine.
2.2 mi.	The trail splits. Stay on the trail to the right for a relatively easy ride along the bluff.
3.6 mi.	From this overlook of the Mississippi River Valley, you may try to look for birds including; bald eagles, trumpeter swans, red-tailed hawks and northern harriers. The Mississippi River corridor is one of the most active areas for bird migrations
4.4 mi.	Take the narrow trail to the left. (If you end up in a cornfield you know you have missed the turn.) Remember the long climb up? Now get ready for a wild descent of nearly a mile. My novice riding partner used the "Fred Flintstone" technique of braking.
5.1 mi.	At the bottom you are exhilarated, only to find you have to climb back up. Pedal on an old field road to the right for .5 miles. In the fall, lush green pastures contrast sharply against the rusty hues of the oaks and hickorys that cover the valley walls.
5.6mi.	To the left is a grassy parking area. Pedal past the gate and up the hill. The climb is tough but will not seem nearly as bad as the first hill.
6.3 mi.	Stay left on top of the bluff for 1.2 miles. Ride through young stands of red oak until you come to the spot where the first climb ended. Turn left and descend the steep trail. It is a blast, but be careful on rocky, washed-out sections of the trail. You may want to do the 1.1mi Trout Creek Loop at the end of the ride.

Trout Valley Trail

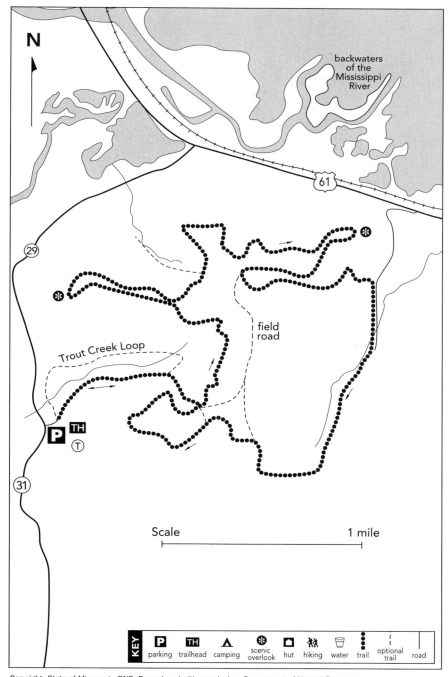

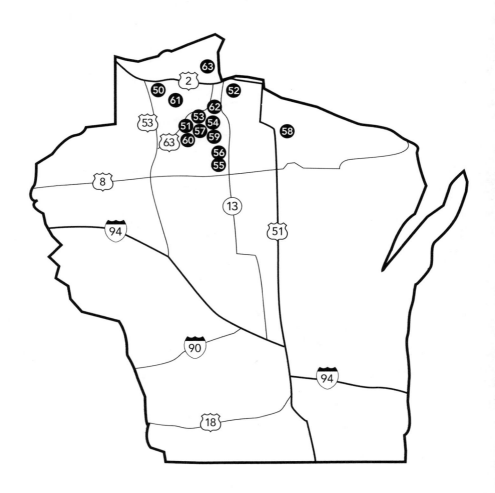

The North Country Guide to
Mountain Biking

SECTION 4

Northern Wisconsin

50   After Hours Ski Trail

51   Bar Stool Loop - CAMBA

52   Copper Falls State Park

53   Drummond Loop - CAMBA

54   Fire Tower Loop - CAMBA

55   Flambeau River State Forest

56   Oxbo Ski Trail

57   Patsy Lake Loop - CAMBA

58   Razorback Ridges

59   Rock Lake - CAMBA

60   Sleigh Trail - CAMBA

61   Tall Pines Loop - CAMBA

62   The North Country Trail

63   Valkyrie North Trail

After Hours Ski Trail
Brule, WI   (715) 372-4866

Distance: 5 miles   **Trail:** Loop on grassy ski trail
Ride Time: 1 hour   **Rating:** Easy to Moderate

Access: A half mile west of Brule, WI on U.S. Hwy 2 to After Hours Road. Look for the parking lot immediately on the left side of the road. No facilities available.

After Hours Ski Trail, located adjacent to Brule River, is famous for its exceptional trout fishing and canoeing. This area was discovered by Daniel Greysolon, Sieur du Lhut, in 1680. The river served as a link between Lake Superior and the Mississippi River. A state trail pass is required to use these trails.

0.0 mi.   Go around the gate. You are at a 3-way intersection. Turn right onto the far right trail. Be cautious of a steep downhill. Stay to the right through the next intersection.

0.3 mi.   Trail splits. Go left to continue on the ski trail.

0.5 mi.   Turn right. Immediately go left at the next intersection. (It is not well marked.) Ride on a nicely wooded trail, Main Street.

0.6 mi.   Turn right off of Main Street onto a section called Triangle Loop. Pedal .3 miles. At the first "you are here" sign, veer right and venture on the West Loop.

1.3 mi.   Ride across an unnamed road that is absolutely gorgeous in the fall. A canopy of maples provides brilliant color.

1.4 mi.   This is another unmarked intersection. Turn left to continue on West Loop. Straight ahead brings you to After Hours Road.

1.5 mi.   Ride straight ahead. The left trail is an alternate loop that rejoins the main trail in .1 miles.

1.7 mi.   Go around the gate and cross the same dirt road you crossed before. Climb a short hill and come to the junction of West and Porcupine Loops. Turn right onto Porcupine Loop.

2.3 mi.   At the junction of Porcupine Loop and Main Street, turn right onto Main Street. Pedal straight ahead through the next two intersections and cross a dirt road. You will be riding towards the Brule River.

2.7 mi.   Scenic overlook. "Little Joe Rapids" is named after Little Joe who capsized his canoe at this point in the 1800's.

3.0 mi.   After a short rise, come to the junction of Little Joe Loop and a new trail called River Loop. Turn right onto River Loop. Be adventurous. This short section is very rough but has great views above the Brule River.

3.6 mi.   Join Pine Loop by taking a right. The going gets a little easier. The grassy trail with gentle climbs still makes for some resistance.

4.1 mi.   Need a bathroom break? Pit toilet provided. This is Main Junction. Veer right onto Main Street and continue straight through next intersection.

4.4 mi.   Turn right. Stay to the right through the next two intersections.

4.7 mi. Be cautious, there is a downhill with a bridge that crosses a creek at the bottom. The alternate trail comes in from your left. Go straight.

5.0 mi. Back at the parking lot. This ride is short enough that it can be combined with an afternoon of canoeing or fishing on the Brule River. Rentals of canoes are available in Brule.

After Hours Ski Trail

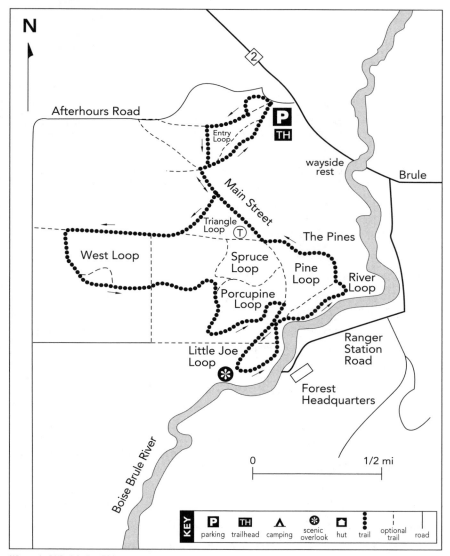

Wisconsin DNR P.O. Box 7921 Madison, Wisconsin 53707 (608) 266-2181

Bar Stool - CAMBA
Hayward, WI   (800) 533-7454

Distance: 15.5 miles
Ride Time: 2-3 hours

Trail: Single-track, ski and snowmobile trails, logging roads
Rating: Easy to Moderate

Access: From Hayward, WI take US Highway 63 north 10 miles to County Road OO. Go east on OO three miles to the trailhead. Look for Kortelopet building.

This ride is a combination of trails from CAMBA's new mountain bike system. You'll enjoy riding on the famous Birkebeiner Ski Trail which meanders through the rolling hills of Namakagon Valley. You are treated to sections of single-track through dense forest. Look for huge stumps along the way that serve as a reminder of the logging days of the 1920's.

0.0 mi.   There are toilets, drinking water, pay phones and picnic benches at the OO trailhead. Begin your ride on the Birkie Ski Trail just beyond the log warming hut.

1.3 mi.   Look for a caution sign alerting you to a snowmobile crossing. Continue straight ahead on the Birkie Ski Trail. (Snowmobile trails cross the Birkie trail at 3.0 and 3.5 miles)

4.3 mi.   There is a blue CAMBA trail marking on the left side of the Birkie trail at this intersection, marked H12. Turn left onto CAMBA's Bar Stool Loop.

4.6 mi.   At jct. H13 go right onto one of the most exciting sections of the trail. This section truly defines what mountain bike riding is all about; a narrow single-track tightly winding through wooded terrain.

5.4 mi.   Emerge into a logged area and join a logging road. Follow the road to the left.

5.8 mi.   At jct. H14 turn right onto Gravel Pit Road.

6.3 mi.   Be aware of a fork in the road. Take the right fork to continue on Gravel Pit Road. The left fork is an active logging road.

6.8 mi.   Cross the Birkie Ski Trail at jct. H7. Pedal .1 miles to jct. H8. Turn left at the intersection of Gravel Pit Road and Phipps Fire Lane.

7.3 mi.   Take a right onto CAMBA's Plantation Loop (H9). This is a bit sandy.

8.6 mi.   At jct. H10 turn left. You are back on Phipps Fire Lane. Pedal past jct. H11. This section of Phipps Fire Lane has challenging areas of deep sugar sand.

11.3 mi. Take a sharp left turn at jct. S22. The trail changes from a wide dirt road to a narrow snowmobile trail. You are now on CAMBA's Frost Pocket Loop. Frost pockets are huge pot holes created by melting chunks of ice left behind by the retreating glacial ice sheet.

11.8 mi. Make a sharp right hand turn at jct. S23. Stay alert! Ahead are steep technical downhills with loose gravel. The last .5 miles of this section is an uphill grind!

13.6 mi. Turn right at S1 for a short easy ride back to Highway OO.

14.4 mi. Turn right onto the pavement (S24) and back to the trailhead.

Bar Stool - CAMBA

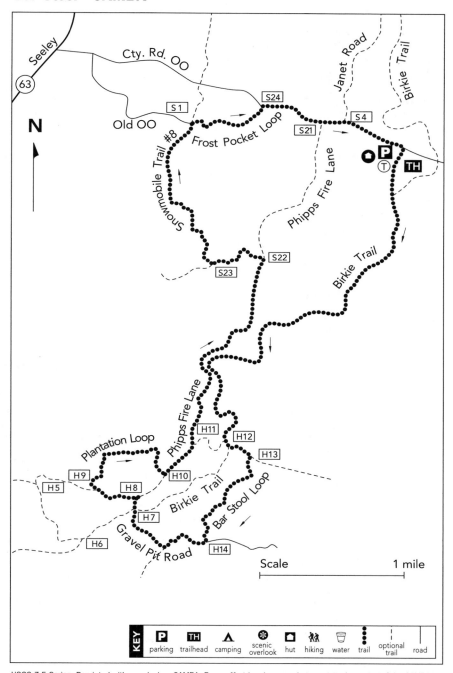

USGS 7.5 Series, Reprinted with permission, CAMBA. Every effort has been made to portray the routes of the CAMBA system as accurate. Changes in the routes may exist now or in the future. For a complete set of maps contact: Chequamegon Area Mountain Bike Association, P.O. Box 141, Cable, WI 54821.

Copper Falls State Park
Mellen, WI (715) 274-5123

Distance: 7 miles
Ride time: 1-2 hours

Trail: Grassy ski trail
Rating: Easy to Moderate

Access: From Ashland, WI take Highway 13, 27 miles south. Before Mellen turn north on Hwy. 169. Soon after, turn west on Co. Rd. J. Road will end at the park office. Daily park permit and trail pass is required.

Copper Falls State Park is named for the 29 foot water fall that marks the first drop in Bad River. The park and falls area was the site of a copper mining camp in the 1860's when there became an increased demand for copper during the Civil War. The varying rock types make these gorges and waterfalls some of the most beautiful in Wisconsin.

0.0 mi. From the park office ride up the road .25 miles and look for the trail on the right side of the road shortly after the ball fields. The trail will split immediately. Stay to the right on the mountain bike/ski trail. To the left is the North Country hiking trail.

0.5 mi. Stay to the right at this intersection. Note a trail merges from the left.

0.7 mi. Ride ahead on Takessian ski loop. To the left is a shortcut.

1.4 mi. Stop and take in the scenery overlooking Bad River. The trail becomes more hilly after the overlook.

1.9 mi. The short cut joins from the left.

2.1 mi. At this intersection take the path to the right that winds down to the Red Granite Falls area. This section of trail is through grassy, rolling terrain. The trail straight ahead leads to the park road.

3.0 mi. Cross over a dirt road.

3.2 mi. Veer right onto the single-track trail that leads to Red Granite Falls.

3.6 mi. Take a right, and soon after, another right. Follow the ski trail signs. Listen. You will be able to hear the falls. Cross an old logging road and continue to follow the ski trail signs. There are numerous footpaths that lead down to Red Granite Falls.

4.2 mi. Go right onto the old road you crossed just before the falls. There are numerous spots along this section that provide beautiful vistas.

5.0 mi. Within the next .1 miles make 2 rights for a return via North Country Trail. The next two intersections continue to the right for the outside loop.

5.6 mi. Cross over the park road to the bathhouse and follow the tar path to the right to see Loon Lake. Pedal back across the park road and veer right onto the old tar road that parallels the park road. Ride this just a few yards. Turn left down the gravel road. Look for North Country Trail immediately on your right.

6.0 mi. At this "Y", jog left onto Group Camp Road for 25 yards. Look for the trail on the right. Follow North Country Trail. (Ignore the footpaths on the right.)

6.8 mi. Ride back to the parking lot on the park road. A hike to Copper and Brownstone Falls is a must!

Copper Falls State Park

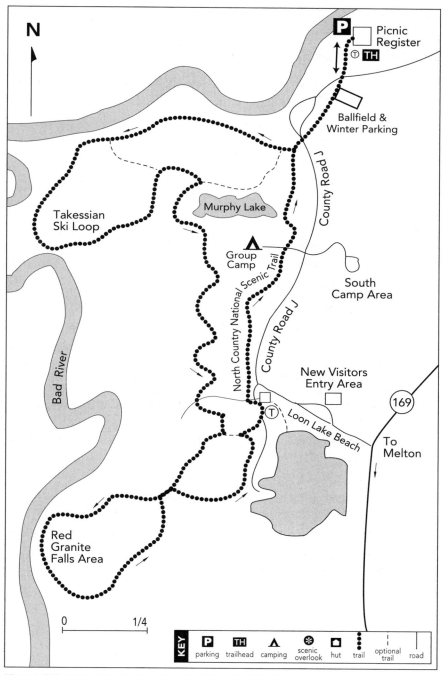

Wisconsin DNR P.O. Box 7921 Madison, Wisconsin 53707 (608) 266-2181

Drummond Loop - CAMBA
Drummond, WI   (800) 533-7454

Distance: 7 .5 miles
Ride time: 1-1.5 hours

Trail: Grassy ski trail, double-track loop
Rating: Moderate

Access: Just north of Drummond, WI on Hwy. 63. Turn east on FR 213 for .9 miles. The ski trail parking lot is located on the north side of FR 213.

Antler/Jack Rabbit/ Boulevard loops have been combined to provide you with the greatest amount of fat tire riding this cluster has to offer. These are the Drummond cross country ski trails. They take you through a mixture of beautiful pine trees and mixed hardwoods.

0.0 mi.	Pick up the trail on the east end of the parking lot. In a short distance, there will be a trail to your right. This is Race Track Loop, opened in 1994. Go straight for the suggested loop.
0.3 mi.	A trail comes in from your left, (D10). Continue straight ahead through beautiful tall pines. Pedal .1 miles and ride through jct. D11.
0.9 mi.	Cross "North Country National Scenic Hiking Trail."
1.3 mi.	At the "Y" intersection turn right (south) on Boulevard Trail, (D12).
1.7 mi.	Veer left (east). Notice the change from pines to mixed hardwoods.
2.0 mi.	Cross back over North Country Hiking Trail. Pedal .5 miles and veer left.
3.0 mi.	At D14, cross over Lake Owen Drive and ride down to the picnic area to enjoy a dip in beautiful, clear Lake Owen. Drinking water and restrooms are available. Ride north out of the picnic area. Stay on Boulevard loop. Retrace your path crossing over North Country Trail. Take a right and cross over the hiking trail again. One more right and you are back to the intersection of Boulevard and Jack Rabbit.
5.2 mi.	Veer right at D12 and ride northeast. Beware of a short, difficult section of trail that can be rough and bumpy.
6.0 mi.	The trail "Y's", Turn left and ride west.
6.5 mi.	Cross North Country Trail and ride through the deep woods. Pedal .3 miles. The Antler Loop will intersect from the left. Continue to ride straight ahead.
7.0 mi.	There will be an unmarked trail at the "Y" intersection. Turn left and ride south.
7.5 mi.	Intersect the main Boulevard Trail at a "T" intersection. Take a right and return back to the ski trail parking lot.

Drummond Loop - CAMBA

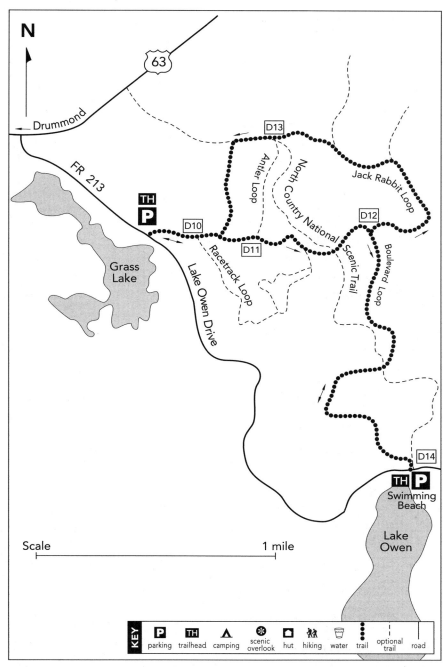

USGS 7.5 Series , Reprinted with permission , CAMBA , Every effort has been made to portray the routes of the CAMBA system as accurate. Changes in the routes may exist now or in the future. For a complete set of maps contact: Chequamegon Area Mountain Bike Association , P.O. Box 141, Cable, WI 54821.

Fire Tower - CAMBA
Seeley, WI   (800) 533-7454

Distance: 12.6 miles
Ride time: 1.5-2 hours

Trail: Logging roads, snowmobile trails
Rating: Easy to Moderate

Access: From Hayward, WI take Highway 63 N. 10 miles to County Road OO. Go east on OO three miles to the trailhead. Look for the Kortelopet building.

Our suggested route takes you on sections of Winding Pines Loop, Fire Tower Loop and Lake Helane Loop. These loops traverse the Seeley Hills above the Namakagon River valley. You'll enjoy riding through dense pine forests, with an opportunity to visit the sight of an old fire tower for spectacular views of the valley.

0.0 mi.   From the trailhead ride west back toward Seeley.

0.5 mi.   At Janet Road (S4), turn right and pedal north on the dirt road.

1.8 mi.   Ride straight ahead going past the S3 trail sign.

2.2 mi.   Climb a slight rise and note the S5 sign. You are now at the intersection of Boedecker and Janet Roads. Turn left and ride a fast section of dirt road.

3.0 mi.   Make a right turn at jct. S6. This section of trail is relatively flat but the riding is much more intimate here through a mixed forest.

3.7 mi.   Cross over the Birkie trail (S7) and continue on Snowmobile 8.

4.5 mi.   After being treated to an easy section at jct. S8, bear left onto Snowmobile Trail 13. Ride past jct. S11 and gradually climb for nearly one mile.

5.4 mi.   You have an option here of turning right at S12 and taking the gentle climb up to the old foundation of Seeley Fire Tower. This scenic overlook has great views of the Namakagon River valley and makes a good picnic spot. Mileage for this side trip: 1 mile. Backtrack down the hill.

6.5 mi.   Ride across the Birkie trail (S13). (There is an old shack on the left side of the trail.)

7.1 mi.   Ride a portion of the Chequamegon Short & Fat race course by taking a right at C20. This is a fun and fast section.

8.0 mi.   Join Fire Tower Loop at S14 by turning right here.

8.4 mi.   Pedal across the Birkie trail again (S15). Stay to your right at S16. Join Lake Helane Loop.

9.3 mi.   "The" Seeley Fire Tower climb (S17)! Would you like to test your climbing skills on this three tier monster? If you visited the old fire tower foundation earlier in the ride, pedal past jct. S17 and save your legs for more riding.

9.8 mi.   Make a quick left turn at jct. S11. Ride straight ahead on Snowmobile Trail 13 (S8) heading south.

10.6 mi.   At Boedecker Rd. (S9) turn right and pedal on an easy rolling section of dirt road.

11.0 mi.   Do you feel like you have crossed the Birkie trail before (S10)?

11.5 mi. Turn left and backtrack on Janet Road (S5), riding south. Go .4 miles past trail sign S3 and finish this section of Janet Road.

13.1 mi. You are now back at Co. Rd. OO. Ride .5 miles east back to the trailhead.

Fire Tower - CAMBA

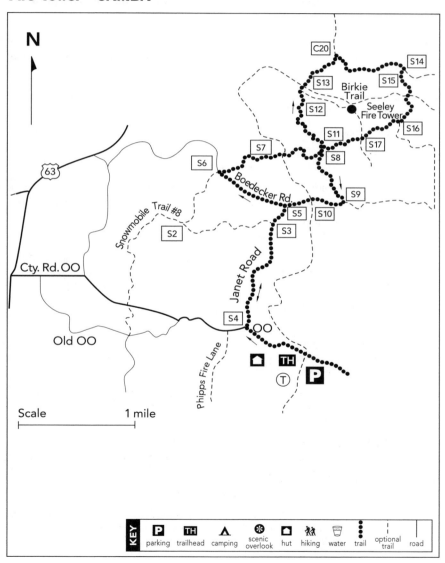

USGS 7.5 Series , Reprinted with permission , CAMBA , Every effort has been made to portray the routes of the CAMBA system as accurate. Changes in the routes may exist now or in the future. For a complete set of maps contact: Chequamegon Area Mountain Bike Association , P.O. Box 141, Cable, WI 54821.

Flambeau River State Forest
Winter, WI **(715) 332-5271**

Distance: 16.5 miles
Ride Time: 3-4 hours

Trail: Single-track on skiing/hiking trails
Rating: Easy to Advanced

Access: From Spooner WI, take highway 70 east, 50 miles, to Winter, WI. From Winter go 19 miles east on Highway 70 to the Oxbo Ski Trail parking lot.

The Flambeau River State Forest is a challenge due to the hilly terrain on the eastern side. Along with the beautiful hardwoods which canopy the trail, there are many scenic points of interest. The beautiful Flambeau River at Pinery Grade is a great picnic place. Include the Oxbo Trail to make a full day trip.

0.0 mi.   Start by taking the 2 mile long Snuss Trail, which starts across highway 70 from the parking lot.

1.9 mi.   Cross Snuss Blvd. and continue on the Snuss Trail. (There is a trail map here.)

3.8 mi.   At this unmarked intersection veer right to stay on the Snuss Trail. Pedal .5 miles and cross Mason Creek. This is a great spot to relax and look for wildlife.

4.6 mi.   Take a right turn, and join Ridge Run. (Note the trail map.) Pedal .75 miles to a four-way intersection. Turn right. Look for the Flambeau River along this section.

5.4 mi.   Turn right to join the Pinery Grade Trail. At the next intersection turn right for a picnic area with shelter or continue on the suggested route.

6.2 mi.   Take a right against the ski sign traffic. You are on the western portion of Rim Creek. In a short distance cross a bridge. There may be wet sections along here due to a beaver's handiwork. Be prepared to portage your bike.

7.8 mi.   Veer right onto the Short Swing Loop. Pedal to the first intersection and veer right.

8.3 mi.   At the "Y" go right for restrooms or left to continue on the Short Swing Loop. Notice the Klug Memorial at the "Y" intersection. Pedal .3 miles staying to the right. Ride past a cutoff path to your left.

9.4 mi.   Cross Rim Creek again on the east side of the Rim Creek Loop. Stay to your right and ride against the ski traffic signs. The topography changes and there are steep downhills ahead.

10.1 mi.   A trail joins from the left. Ride straight, onto the hilly Squirrel Trail. Pedal 1.5 miles to the junction of Ridge Run and Snuss Trail. Turn right onto Snuss Trail.

12.1 mi.   Cross back over Mason Creek. Ride .4 miles.and note a spur trail on the right. Continue on Snuss Trail by veering slightly left.

14.4 mi.   Cross over the dirt road. The trail makes a small loop and crosses Snuss Blvd. You can take a left and follow the gravel road 1.5 miles back to the trailhead. If not, backtrack on the Snuss Trail 1.9 miles.

Flambeau River State Forest

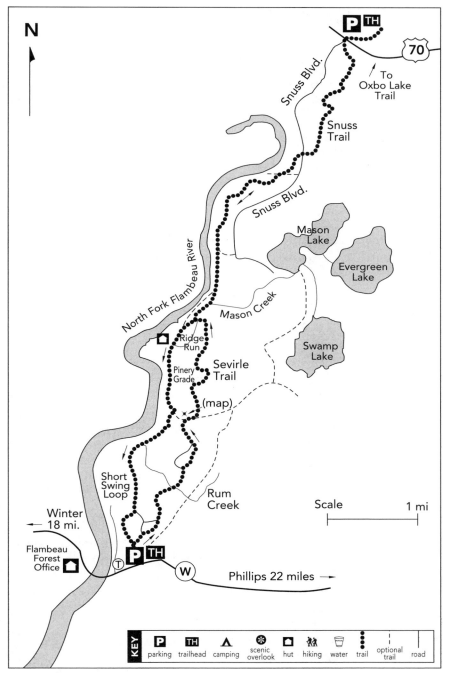

Wisconsin DNR P.O. Box 7921 Madison, Wisconsin 53707 (608) 266-2181.

147

Oxbo Ski Trail
Draper, WI   (715) 332-5271

Distance: 7.2 miles   **Trail:** Loop on grassy ski trails
Ride Time: 1- 1.5 hours   **Rating:** Easy to Moderate

Access: From Spooner, WI take Highway 70 east, 60 miles to Draper, WI. From Draper continue 9 miles east on Highway 70 to the Oxbo Ski Trail. Parking lot is on the north side of the road.

The North Fork of the Flambeau River flows near the Oxbo Trail System. Wildlife such as ospreys, bald eagles, deer, black bear, and otters can be seen along the tree lined shores of the river. Amenities are available at the Oxbo Resort.

0.0 mi.	The trails begin at the northeast corner of the parking lot next to the trailhead information board. Ride .1 miles to a "Y". Turn right to join loop #1.
0.3 mi.	Turn left. You will be pedaling through a plantation pine forest. Look for the hiking sign on the right side of the trail.
0.6 mi.	At this "Y" intersection, veer to your left. In a short distance notice another trail sign in a tree to the right side of the trail.
1.4 mi.	Choose the trail on your right to stay on the eastern perimeter of loop #2.
1.9 mi.	Come to a "T" intersection. Turn right to join loop #3. The forest here is mostly northern hardwoods.
2.1 mi.	Ride to your right and look for the blue ski sign on the tree. Pedal .3 miles, stay left and skip loop #4. Veer left and continue to follow loop #3 signs.
2.6 mi.	Loop #4 rejoins loop #3 at this point. Ride straight ahead for .3 miles and join loop #5 by veering to your right at the "T". Oxbo Lake lies between this section of trail and the Flambeau River.
3.3 mi.	Caution! At the bottom of this steep hill, you have to portage your bike about 25 yards across a bog. The left side is higher and drier.
3.7 mi.	Take the single-track trail on your right down to a beautiful picnic site on the edge of the Flambeau River. This would make a great camp site. (Overnight camping requires a permit that can be obtained at the forest headquarters.) Backtrack up to the main trail to continue the ride.
3.8 mi.	Turn left here and look for the blue ski signs.
4.3 mi.	Pedal ahead to rejoin the west side of loop 3. Ride a short distance and cross an overgrown trail. Climb a small ridge and follow the ski signs.
4.6 mi.	At the "T" take the trail to the right. In .1 miles you will cross that same overgrown trail. This section of loop #3 is rough and perfect for the adventurous rider.
5.0 mi.	Veer right and climb a small rise. Pedal .3 miles and continue on loop #3 by turning left. (The right trail takes you to Oxbo Resort.)
5.5 mi.	Follow the ski signs to the right. Pedal .1 miles and select the trail to your right. Ride against the directional ski signs.
6.0 mi.	Finish the ride on the west side of loop #1, by choosing the right hand trail.

Oxbo Ski Trail

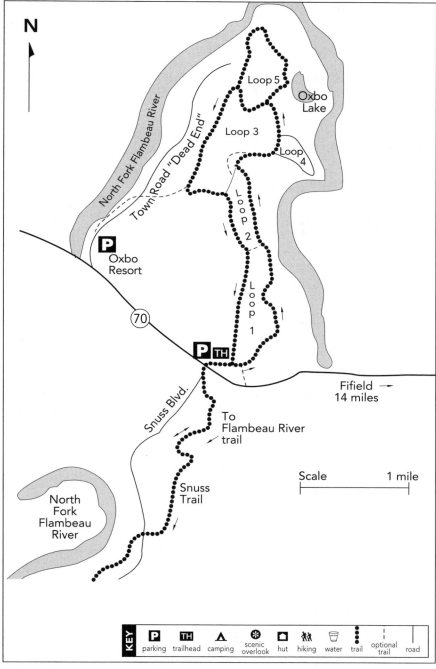

N

Loop 5

Oxbo Lake

Loop 3

Loop 4

North Fork Flambeau River

Town Road "Dead End"

Loop 2

P
Oxbo Resort

70

Loop 1

P TH

Fifield →
14 miles

Snuss Blvd.

To Flambeau River trail

Snuss Trail

North Fork Flambeau River

Scale   1 mile

KEY	P	TH	▲	✳	◻	🚶	⊔	⋮	┆	—
	parking	trailhead	camping	scenic overlook	hut	hiking	water	trail	optional trail	road

Wisconsin DNR P.O. Box 7921 Madison, Wisconsin 53707 (608) 266-2181.

Patsy Lake - CAMBA
Namakagon, WI   (800) 533-7454

Distance: 13 miles   **Trail:** Dirt road, double-track, some single-track
Ride time: 2-2.5 hours   **Rating:** Easy to Moderate

Access: From Highway 63 in Cable, WI, take Highway M east 10 miles. Turn south just past the Highway D intersection and enter the Namakagon Town Hall parking lot. No amenities available.

The Patsy lake loop is one of the outstanding CAMBA rides through the Chequamegon National Forest. This gently rolling trail passes old growth pines with views of Patsy Lake.

0.0 mi.   The Namakagon trailhead is behind the town hall. Ride south on FR 200 for .5 miles. Turn right on Snowmobile 8.

1.2 mi.   Bear right at the fork N1. Pedal 1 mile to the intersection of Snowmobile 3 and Patsy Lake Loop. At jct. N2 turn left and ride less then .1 mile on an overgrown single-track. At N19 turn right on the single-track.

2.6 mi.   Turn right at a dirt road. Pedal .1 mile and turn left on FR 203 for 100 feet. Then take a right on a two-track trail at N20. Bear right through the next two intersections.

3.8 mi.   Descend a short hill and turn right. Pedal .1 mile and cross a two-track trail. At intersection N21 go right on the dirt two-track.

4.4 mi.   At jct. N22 bear left up a slight hill. At jct. N13 go left for .3 miles. Take a right onto a narrow, technical, single-track which takes you around a wet area. You will be treated to a great picnic spot and a view of Patsy Lake.

4.9 mi.   Cross a beaver dam on planks that are slippery when wet.

5.0 mi.   Take advantage of the clearing to view Patsy Lake. Leave the clearing on a trail that parallels the shore. There is one small water crossing on this section of trail.

5.5 mi.   Pass a small lake with several wood duck houses. At jct. N14 there is a cutoff option to the left. Continue the route by taking a hard right.

5.7 mi.   Turn left just before a clearing. Follow the trail to the left through a second clearing. Continue on the rolling two-track. Ride .5 miles. Come to an intersection and veer left.

6.5 mi.   Reach a fork at which you bear left again. In .1 miles turn left onto double-track. Cruise .4 miles and go right onto FR 206 at jct. N23. At jct. N24 bear left.

7.7 mi.   Come to a "T" with Snowmobile Trail 3 at jct. N25. There are a few washout areas here. Turn left at N25 onto Snowmobile Trail 3. Ride through pine forest on double-track along the edge of occasional clear cuts.

8.7 mi.   Turn right at an intersection with another two track. In .2 miles cross FR 203 and continue northeast on a short, bumpy section of single-track.

9.0 mi.   At jct. N16, a double-track; turn right.

9.8 mi.   At N17 the two-track intersects with the Namakagon loop. Go straight .4 miles. Veer left, then continue to ride north by going slightly right.

10.7 mi. Turn right at N19. At jct. N2 veer right and back track north to N1. Continue straight ahead at N1 for nearly 2 miles. Turn left onto FR 200 back to the trailhead.

Patsy Lake - CAMBA

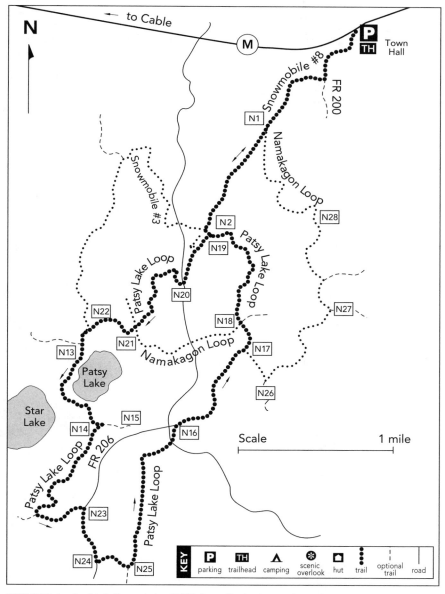

USGS 7.5 Series, Reprinted with permission, CAMBA, Every effort has been made to portray the routes of the CAMBA system as accurate. Changes in the routes may exist now or in the future. For a complete set of maps contact: Chequamegon Area Mountain Bike Association , P.O. Box 141, Cable, WI 54821.

Razorback Ridges
Sayner, WI (715) 542-3019 (715) 542-3818

Distance: 10-12 miles
Ride time: 1-2 hours

Trail: Two-track and single-track
Rating: Moderate to Advanced

Access: From Minoqua/Woodruff WI, go north on Hwy. 51 five miles to County Road M. Drive north approximately two miles to County Road N head east for seven miles. Turn left onto Razorback Road and park at McKay's Corner Store

Razorback Ridges is home to Ridge Rider WORS (Wisconsin Off-Road Series) Mountain bike race held in late August. The terrain is varied and provides all levels of ability for riders. For more information on Razorback Ridges Trail system call the Chamber of Commerce at 715-542-3789.

Looking at McKay's store, the trails start just to the right; ride across their property to access the main trail. Cruise past the first three intersections. Follow the Old Timers to Long Rider.

Turn off onto Black Bears Run, a nice single-track offshoot. Return to Long Rider and take a left. Just past the Mary's Frolic intersection turn left onto a technical expert section. This section will join Snomo's trail and give you views of Muskellunge Lake.

Cut over from Snomo's trail to Blueberry Lake Loop, you will find a dock that overlooks this charming lake. Continue on past the boat landing and ride on Beaver's Run, an expert level single-track that crosses Long Rider trail.

Once you cross Long Rider trail it becomes Rattle Snake, this trail will give both your granny gear and your brakes a workout!

Rattle Snake turns into Bruce's Mountain which literally dumps you back out to Long Rider. Pedal to the right against traffic to Corkscrew and over to Mary's Frolic. Hang a left onto Mary's Frolic and up to Long Rider.

Take a left on Long Rider and a quick right on Duck Lake Loop.
After Duck Lake Loop turn left onto Buck Ridge and ride this trail to Long Rider. Follow Long Rider back down past Ridge Trail and Old Timers back to Mckay's Corner Store for some well deserved refreshments.

*The ambiguity of the map and lack of accurate trail markings make it nearly impossible to give you perfect mileage and directions. However, think of it as just adding to the adventure.

Razorback Ridges

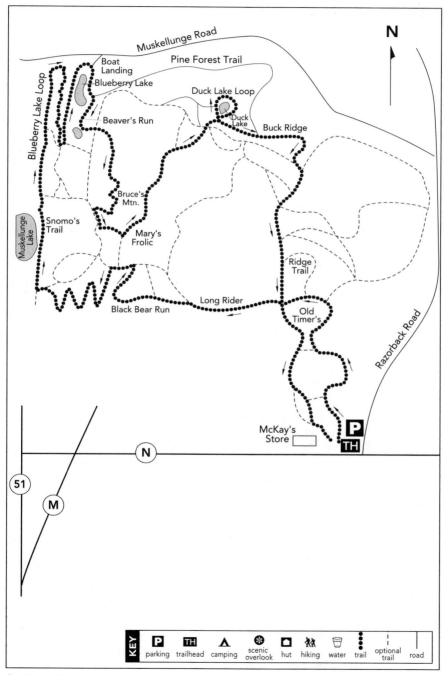

Reprinted with permission from Sayner-Star Lake Lions Club

Rock Lake - CAMBA
Cable, WI   (800) 533-7454

Distance: 10 miles
Ride time: 2 hours

Trail: Single-track loop through deep forest
Rating: Moderate to Advanced

Access: From Hayward, WI follow Hwy 63 north 17 miles to Cable. Go east on Co. Rd. M 7.5 miles to the Rock Lake trailhead. Ammenities available at Glacier Pines Outfitters.

The best roller coaster ride on a bike! The 10 mile Rock Lake trail through Chequamegon National Forest is one of the best single-track rides in the Midwest. It is beautiful as well as technically challenging. The many trails in this system allow several options for difficulty and length.

0.0 mi.   Pick up the trail near the map board. The trail is marked with blue diamonds and CAMBA signs. Pedal .5 miles and cross the first of many logging roads.

0.5 mi.   Turn right to continue on the long loop. (Ignore the 2km cut off and Glacier Pines Trail to the left.)

0.8 mi.   At trail marker N7 continue to the right.

1.3 mi.   At the 4km cut off stay on the main trail. Pedal up to a logging road, and veer left with a quick jog to the right around a gate. Keep a look-out for trail markers.

1.5 mi.   Stay right at N8 where Rock Lake Trail and Glacier Trail intersect. (This is also the 7km cutoff.)

2.0 mi.   Ride past the trail on your right. You will see a fire ring and crystal clear Rock Lake. This is a perfect spot for a dip on a hot day. Pedal .5 miles on the south side of Rock Lake.

2.5mi.   Veer left here unless you wish to ride completely around Rock Lake. Soon after the intersection is the 11.5km cut off. Go straight ahead for the suggested ride. If you want to avoid the most challenging climbs take the 11.5km cutoff.

3.1 mi.   A trail merges from the left. Stay to the right. The route is much less traveled beyond the 11.5km cutoff point and is dotted with small lakes.

4.0 mi.   The route "Y's". The logging road goes straight. Take the trail to the left and pedal into the woods for more roller coaster riding.

5.0 mi.   Cross over FR 207 (N29). For the next two miles there are many small trails and logging roads that criss-cross the main trail. Be observant and you will not get lost. The back section of the trail passes several lakes and climbs over several steep ridges. Ride past N30.

6.3 mi.   The 11.5km loop merges from the left. Continue to the right. Ride through junction N11. Pedal 2 miles. The 7km loop joins from the left.

9.0 mi.   The trail crosses back over FR 207 (N6). Go around the gate. Pedal .3 miles. The 4km trail joins from the left. Pedal .8 miles to a potentially confusing intersection. Cross over a snowmobile trail and the single-track where the ride started. Pedal .2 miles back to the trailhead.

Rock Lake - CAMBA

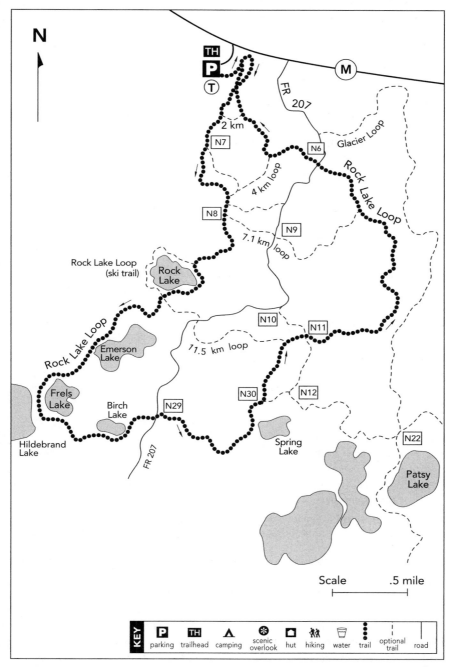

USGS 7.5 Series , Reprinted with permission , CAMBA , Every effort has been made to portray the routes of the CAMBA system as accurate. Changes in the routes may exist now or in the future. For a complete set of maps contact: Chequamegon Area Mountain Bike Association , P.O. Box 141, Cable, WI 54821.

Sleigh Trail - CAMBA
Cable, WI   (800) 533-7454

Distance: 11.7 miles   **Trail:** Ski trails, single-track and logging roads
Ride time: 2 hours   **Rating:** Easy to Moderate

Access: From Hayward, WI, take Hwy. 63 north 17 miles to Cable, WI. Go east on Co. Rd. M 2.5 miles to Telemark Rd. Proceed south to Telemark Resort. Follow the road behind the lodge and park by the tennis courts.

Ride through the pristine, Bayfield County forest on narrow single-tracks, old sleigh trails, logging roads, and the Birkie trail. Amenities available at Telemark Resort. Telemark Property has undergone extensive logging, so this map will not be up-to-date. Please stop for the most current map at Telemark lodge. Our maps will be updated when logging is completed.

0.0 mi.   Follow the dirt road to the left at the west end of the lot. Ride 1/2 block and turn right onto the far right hand trail, marked "Trailhead". (Do not ride on undesignated Telemark trails.)

0.2 mi.   Where the trail splits, go left riding against the ski traffic signs.

0.8 mi.   At C19 take a hard right and ride past the warming hut. Come to a 3-way intersection. Take the middle trail, a wonderful single-track section called Nature Trail.

1.4 mi.   Go left at C18. The trail widens. At C17 take a sharp right up a short, steep hill onto Sleigh Trail. Continue straight ahead under the powerline.

3.0 mi.   Pedal across an unmarked logging road.

3.5 mi.   Randysek Road is on your right. (Trail map C3 is located across the dirt road.) Stay on the grassy trail that winds up and joins the powerline. Ride the power line for only a short distance.

3.6 mi.   Make a sharp right onto the famous Birkebeiner Ski Trail. This section of the Birkie rolls through mixed hardwood forests.

4.8 mi.   Cross an unmarked logging road and continue on the "Birkie." At CAMBA marker C14 continue straight ahead.

5.5 mi.   Continue straight at C13. Pass a trail coming in from your right. Continue on this roller coaster section of the "Birkie."

6.5 mi.   Make a right (C6) onto a dirt road called Timber Trail. Pedal 1 mile and turn right onto Randysek Road, also called Snowmobile 13. Pedal a short distance. Take a right (C4) onto a single-track. Be careful of a steep descent and a tricky turn at the bottom of the hill. Ride on the ridge for beautiful views of the valley.

8.3 mi.   (C13). This "T" intersection is the Birkie trail again. Take a left and back track this section of the Birkie. Grunt back up a short, steep hill.

8.8 mi.   (C14). There is a trail map here. Leave the wide Birkie trail by taking a right turn onto a rolling section of single-track. You are riding on an old horse-drawn sleigh trail used by Telemark Lodge years ago.

9.1 mi.   At C15 turn left and have a blast on this fast and rolling narrow trail. Cross over several trails and follow the CAMBA markers.

10.2 mi. (C16) Turn right onto the Birkie trail. At the 49K marker descend on the "Birkie Roller." At the "T" take a right to continue downhill.

10.7 mi. Put the brakes on and go left onto a bypass that takes you around a potentially deep pond that has swallowed many a biker in wet years.

10.9 mi. (C19) Go left back onto the wide main Birkie trail and follow CAMBA markers back to the original dirt road. Take a left on the dirt road back to the parking lot.

Sleigh Trail - CAMBA

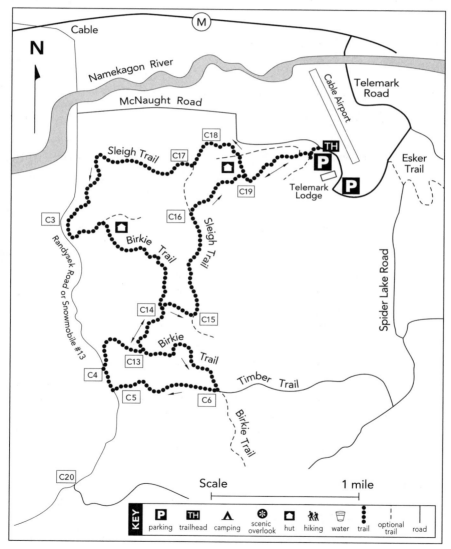

USGS 7.5 Series, Reprinted with permission, CAMBA, Every effort has been made to portray the routes of the CAMBA system as accurate. Changes in the routes may exist now or in the future. For a complete set of maps contact: Chequamegon Area Mountain Bike Association , P.O. Box 141, Cable, WI 54821.

Tall Pines - CAMBA
Iron River, WI   (800) 533-7454

Distance: 21.3 miles
Ride time: 2.5-3 hours

Trail: Single-track, dirt, and logging roads
Rating: Moderate

Access: From Cable go north on U.S. Highway 63. Turn east onto County Road N. Turn north on County Road A to the trailhead sign on the right side of the road. From Iron River go five miles south to the trailhead.

Tall Pines Loop offers views of large red and white pines. This area is used by migrating timber wolves from the Rainbow Lake Wilderness area pack. There are efforts to reduce the road density in this area which can only enhance the deep-woods riding experience. Bring plenty of food and water. There is a new trailhead off FR 229, but we will continue to use the North Country Hiking Trail.

0.0 mi.	The trailhead is marked as North Country Hiking Trail. Ride on rolling terrain of this hiking trail past a small pond on your right. Pedal .75 mile and turn right onto a dirt road W30 leaving the North Country trail.
1.7 mi.	Stay to your left on the Barrons loop. Pedal one mile. You encounter a very sandy section here. Veer left on the CAMBA trail for a short bypass around deep sand.
3.0 mi.	Take a right and ride on FR411 through a tall pine forest. Cruise through the woods for 1.3 miles. At jct. W3 turn left and join FR412. (Bear with the wide dirt road—it will not last long.)
5.4 mi.	At jct. W14 veer right and follow the signs for Tall Pines Loop. Ride .75 miles and veer right again onto W17. Tall Pines Loop is great in July when the wild blueberries and raspberries are ripe for the picking.
6.7 mi.	This intersection may seem confusing because it is unmarked. Continue straight ahead and you will see a CAMBA marker.
7.0 mi.	Turn left onto FR401. Pedal almost .5 miles and turn right onto a logging road. Ride straight ahead on the logging road for 1.6 miles.
8.6 mi.	Go left onto a grassy two-track which turns into a rough section of single-track. Pedal 1 mile and veer right at jct. W5 and join a two-track trail.
10.5 mi.	Turn right onto an obscure logging road at jct W6. This is probably the most scenic part of the trail. Riding through the thick hardwood forest, pedal .3 miles and go left following CAMBA signs.
12.0 mi.	Go left on a two-track road and continue to follow CAMBA signs. Pedal .5 miles and cross FR229. This intersection is the new trailhead for Tall Pines. Proceed straight ahead on a two-track road.
12.6 mi.	Stay to your right on CAMBA marked trails through the next two junctions.
13.6 mi.	Veer left. Continue to ride through a wonderful forested area. Pedal .3 miles. At jct. W7 turn right and head north towards W4.
15.2 mi.	Come to a 4-way junction. Proceed straight ahead on Snowmobile trail #5. This is moderately rolling terrain. Pedal one mile and cross over FR231.

17.4 mi. At jct. W4 ride to the left heading back to the main trailhead.

20.3 mi. Turn left at jct. W1. At the next intersection turn right and ride down the dirt road back to the trailhead. Now is the time for a refreshing swim in Lake Ruth.

Tall Pines - CAMBA

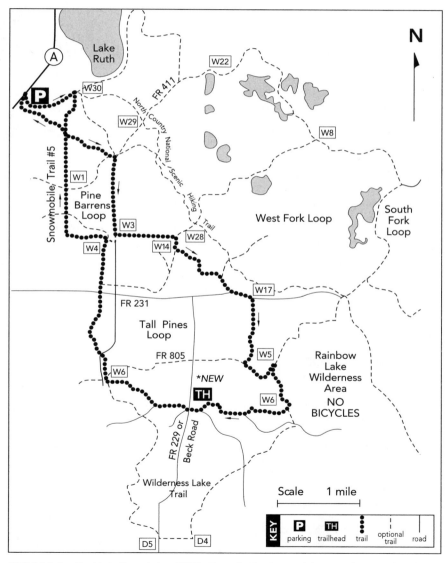

USGS 7.5 Series , Reprinted with permission , CAMBA , Every effort has been made to portray the routes of the CAMBA system as accurate. Changes in the routes may exist now or in the future. For a complete set of maps contact: Chequamegon Area Mountain Bike Association , P.O. Box 141, Cable, WI 54821.

The North Country Trail
Chequamegon National Forest
Hayward, WI   (715) 634-4821

Distance: 14-16 miles   **Trail:** Single-track & forest service roads
Ride time: 2-3 hours   **Rating:** Moderate

Access: From Cable, WI, take Hwy. 63 north to Grandview. Go south on Hwy. D approximately 5 miles. Pass the Great Divide marker on the west side of the road and look for FR201. There will be a parking lot just past FR201 on the west side of Hwy. D. There are no facilities available here so make sure you bring plenty of food and water. Also note the North County Trail to the west of Hwy. D is a designated wilderness area and is off-limits to mountain bikes.

The North Country National Scenic Trail winds its way across the landscape of northern Wisconsin as part of a trail that begins with the grandeur of the Adirondack Mountains of New York and ends in the vast plains of North Dakota. This section of the trail meanders through the ancient Penokee Mountain Range. There are numerous vistas of rock outcroppings, bluffs and many lakes and streams. Look for the Swedish settlement site and if your lucky, the elusive Timber Wolf.

0.0 mi.	Cross over Hwy. D and join this section of trail which is legal to ride on. Any section of the North Country Trail designated as wilderness areas are strictly off limits to mountain biking. Please adhere to this regulation.
0.5 mi.	Cross over FR201. You will be riding through young hardwood stands on an enjoyable single-track.
1.5 mi.	Ride across road 1780 and start looking for markings for the fire tower.
2-2.5 mi.	Between this distance look for an unmarked trail to your left which will take you to Long Mile lookout, a fire tower situated on a high rock outcrop that affords beautiful views, especially in the fall.
3.5 mi.	Cross FR378.
5.0 mi.	You will cross FR202 and find a parking lot here. The topography changes to lowland and marsh for a short while, before climbing up to the Marengo River area. Look for the signs along the trail that direct you to a scenic overlook with sweeping panoramas of the Marengo River Valley that will leave you wondering if you're out west or really in Wisconsin. The Marengo River is a well known trout stream. Continue on down the trail. Cross the river on a well built bridge. Climb out of the valley and come to an intersection where going straight leads you to the adirondack shelter (where you can stay overnight) or go left to visit an old Swedish settlement abandoned in the 1920's. After visiting these sites we suggest backtracking on the single-track to FR202. Turn left on FR202 for approximately 2 miles to FR201. Turn right on FR201. It is approximately 4 miles back to the parking lot. Another option would be to simply ride the North Country Trail back to your car on Hwy. D. If you choose this option the total mileage is around 14 miles and the gravel road option is about 16 miles.

The North Country Trail

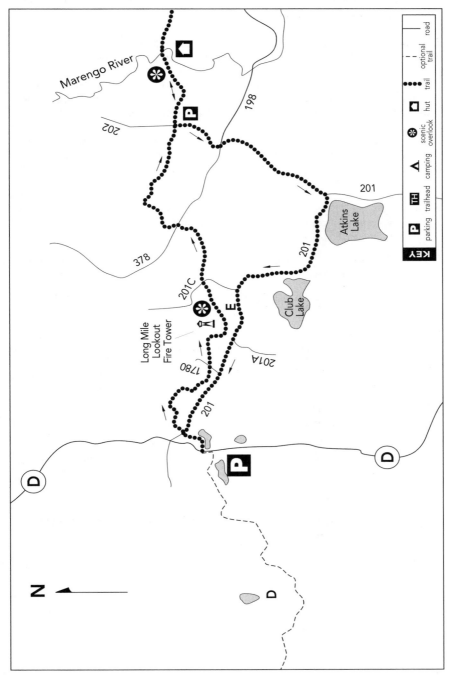

Reprinted with permission from Wisconsin DNR

Valkyrie North Trail
Washburn, WI (715) 373-2667

Distance: 6.4 miles   **Trail:** Loop on grassy ski trail
Ride time: 1-1.5 hours   **Rating:** Moderate to Advanced

Access: From Ashland, WI take Hwy 2 west to Hwy 13. North on Hwy 13 to Washburn. Left on Co. Rd. C, 8 miles to Mt.Valhalla Recreation Area. Go to the west end of the parking lot to the information board. Water not available.

Valkyrie Ski Trail at Mt. Valhalla Recreation Area is located in Chequamegon National Forest. The Valkyrie trail winds through forests of pine, birch and aspen. Ice age glaciers sheared off the tops of hills and filled in valleys, creating rolling terrain. Voyageurs, Fur Traders, Native Americans and Loggers have all left their footprints on this land.

0.0 mi.	Take the FR 439 across from Co. Rd. C, turn immediately to your right onto the Valkyrie Ski Trail. Ride in the direction of the ski trail signs. The trail is lined with majestic pine trees.
0.6 mi.	The trail splits. Take a right onto Loop B. There is a short, steep climb followed by fast downhills.
0.8 mi.	Cross a snowmobile trail. Pedal .1 miles and cross the same snowmobile trail again.
1.3 mi.	At the next trail intersection veer right for .1 miles and cross FR #439. A clear cut area is soon visible. This section is rolling with tight turns.
2.7 mi.	Cross a FR 256. The trail is lined with hardwoods and evergreens. Climb to a ridge that overlooks a pine-filled valley on your left. You are now on loop C.
3.3 mi.	Cross over a snowmobile trail and cruise for 1.1 miles until you come to a tricky turn. Go left, but make sure you follow the ski trail signs that lead you up a short hill.
4.9 mi.	Again, cross the snowmobile trail. There is a mature forest on the right side of the trail.
5.2 mi.	Pedal across a dirt road and plunge downhill on a fast and furious ride.
5.9 mi.	Cross back over FR #439. Stay to the right through the next 3 intersections. This is a nice wooded section of the trail.
6.4 mi.	Trailhead.

Valkyrie North Trail

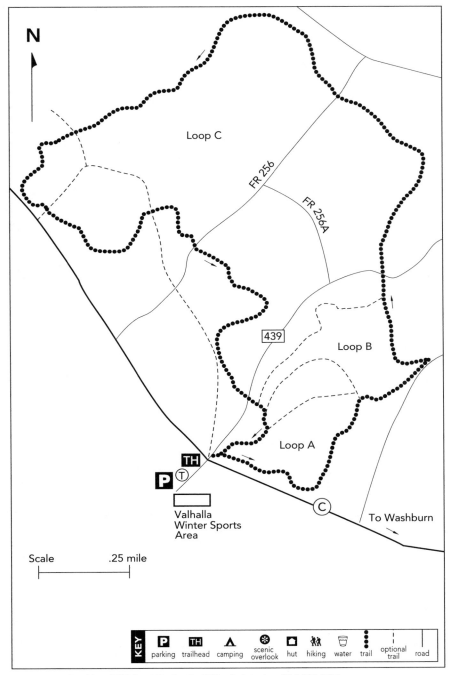

Maps are reproduced from USDA Forest Service Paul Witte, Cartographer (414) 297-3403

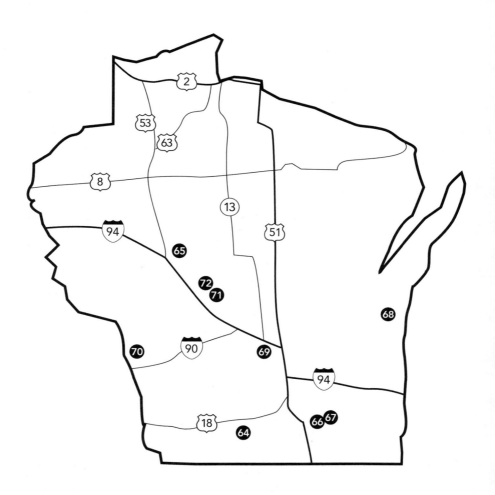

The North Country Guide to
Mountain Biking

SECTION 5

Southern Wisconsin

64   Governor Dodge State Park

65   Lake Wissota State Park

66   Kettle Moraine - Emma Carlin

67   Kettle Moraine - John Muir

68   Kettle Moraine - Northern Unit

69   Mirror Lake State Park

70   Perrot State Park

71   Smrekar Trail - Black River State Forest

72   Wildcat Trail - Black River State Forest

Governor Dodge State Park
Dodgeville, WI   (608) 935-2315

Distance: 10.1 miles   **Trail:** 2 loops of hard-packed dirt
Ride time: 1 hour   **Rating:** Moderate

Access: From Madison, WI go forty miles west on Highway 18. Go north on County Road 23 six miles.

The area that is now southwestern Wisconsin was bypassed by the recent glaciers, leaving an untouched island of steep hills, sandstone bluffs and deep valleys amid the surrounding flat prairies. The park offers 10 miles of moderately challenging fat-tire trails as well as access to the 39 mile long Military Ridge State Trail.

0.0 mi.   Park at Cox Hollow Beach. The trail starts down the hill. Ride along the lake and across an earthen dam. Gradually climb the gravel trail for .5 miles.

0.6 mi.   The trail splits at the top of the hill. Ride to left onto the less traveled trail. Beautiful woods, open meadows and overlooks of several lakes highlight this 3.3 mile loop.

1.0 mi.   As the trail meanders through the woods, the path bends to the right for a beautiful overlook of a small lake. Pedal along the edge of a bluff.

1.8 mi.   The winding trail switchbacks to the left into the woods and downhill. At the bottom, pedal along Mill Creek.

3.3 mi.   Turn right onto the main gravel trail back to the parking lot. The Meadow Valley Trail starts at the northeast end of the parking lot. The trail heads out of the valley with a quarter mile climb up a moderate hill to an open meadow.

4.0mi.   Pedal on 50 ft. of pavement and onto a grassy trail. The trail winds in and out of the trees for .75 miles.

4.7 mi.   Turn left where the trail splits. Climb uphill and cross the park road. The bluff top supports mostly prairie grasses. Cruise downhill through small stands of aspens, maples and oaks.

5.5 mi.   Turn right and follow the Gold Mining Trail. Pedal .3 miles along the ridge. A steep cliff creates a queasy overlook of the river valley.

6.2 mi.   A scenic overlook and bench provide a perfect opportunity for a picnic stop and a chance to pull out the binoculars.

6.7 mi.   Take a right at the "T" in the trail. The trail crosses a road at the top of a small hill and ducks into the woods. The hard-packed trail makes easy riding.

7.1 mi.   The trail splits. Turn right following the edge of the woods until it plunges half a mile down a curved trail to the valley floor. A great ride!!

7.9 mi.   Pick up the trail to the right. Coast down another hill. You can see a lake to your left. A long stretch of sand makes this area tough pedaling.

9.0 mi.   Stay to the left where the trail "Y's". Ride along the lake and up the hill. The trail descends and winds along a marsh. Climb back out of the valley to the parking area.

166

Governor Dodge State Park

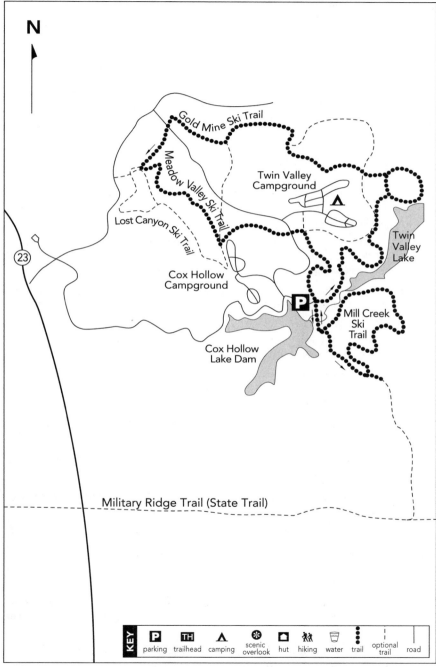

Wisconsin DNR, P.O. Box 7921, Madison, Wisconsin 53707 (608) 266-2181.

Lake Wissota State Park
Chippewa Falls, WI   (715) 382-4574

Distance: 4.6 miles
Ride time: 1 hour

Trail: Loop on ski/hiking trail
Rating: Easy

Access: From Chippewa Falls, WI drive north on Highway 53. Head east on County Road S. There will be signs directing you to the park. At County Road O turn right and drive 1.7 miles to the park entrance. A state park sticker is required for admittance as well as a wheel pass. Park at the beach.

Lake Wissota is situated on a sandy outwash plain formed from deposits of the ancient Chippewa River. Lake Wissota was created when settlers dammed the river at Chippewa Falls at the turn of the century.

0.0 mi.	Ride out of the parking lot and turn left onto the road. Pedal .1 miles and turn right onto the ski trail. Immediately veer right at 3-way intersection to join the Jack Pine Trail.
0.6 mi.	Ride briefly onto the paved road. Turn left immediately back onto the grassy single-track. The Staghorn, Beaver, Meadow and Nature Trails are closed to mountain biking. Please stay on designated trails.
0.7 mi.	Turn left at the junction of the Staghorn and Jack Pine trails. Ride .1 miles and veer right onto the Eagle Prairie Trail. Look for red-tail hawks hunting in the open prairie.
1.2 mi	Bear right at this intersection. Ride .1 miles through open meadows. Cross a horse trail of deep, sugary sand.
1.7 mi.	The topography changes from prairie grass to plantation pines. The pine corridor makes for much more intimate riding. Ride .3 miles and turn right to join the Plantation Trail.
2.8 mi.	Veer right and ride down another corridor of pines. You have just entered the Red Pines Trail also called the Fitness Loop.
3.0 mi.	Stay to your left and ride down the trail carpeted with pine needles. (The trail to your right takes you to the park road.)
3.3 mi.	Where the Red Pine loop ends, turn right and backtrack. Cross the horse trail and ride along the edge of the plantation pines and open prairie.
3.7 mi.	Veer right where the trail "Y's".
3.9 mi.	On your left is an interpretive area that describes the evolution of the prairie as well as animal life that is native to this habitat. Cross over the paved road and ride into a mixed hardwood forest.
4.2 mi.	Turn left at the "T" intersection. (The Lake Trail is closed to mountain biking.) Veer left at the next intersection. We stared down a 12 point buck and a doe here.
4.5 mi.	Turn right at the park road, and go .1 miles back to the parking lot. This ride can be combined with an afternoon of hiking or a swim in Lake Wissota.

Lake Wissota State Park

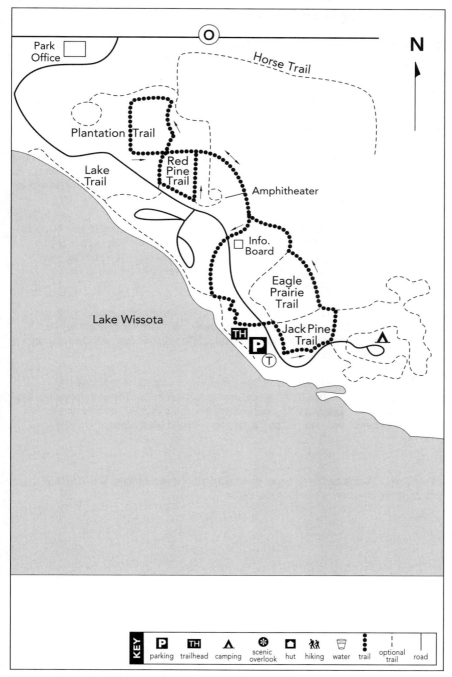

Wisconsin DNR, P.O. Box 7921, Madison, Wisconsin 53707 (608) 266-2181.

Kettle Moraine/Emma F. Carlin
Eagle, WI   (414) 594-2135

Distance: 18.4 miles
Ride time: 2-3 hours

Trail: Hard-packed, single-track
Rating: Moderate to Difficult

Access: From Whitewater, WI take Hwy. 12 east to LaGrange. Turn north on Hwy. H at the general store. Drive past the first parking area up to Bluff Road. Turn left and park. Public parking is allowed here. A daily or annual trail pass is required and can be purchased at LaGrange General Store.

This trail, along with the John Muir trails, are among the most popular in all of Wisconsin. Riders from Milwaukee, Chicago and Madison make the pilgrimage to the Kettle every weekend. The LaGrange General Store at the intersection of 12 and H has great food to stoke you for a full day of riding. Also, full service bike shops can take care of any of your biking needs.

0.0 mi.   Ride east on Bluff Road about 1/4 mile past the intersection of Hwy. H. Look for the connector trail on the left side of the road. This first section of the connector trail is an easy warm-up for what lies ahead. The trail has some steep short climbs. Maintenance of the trail requires the use of erosion control mats on steep grades.

1.5 mi.   Cross over Young Road; watch for traffic. Be careful on this section; this is a busy, tight, 2-way trail. You will cross over two more county roads before coming to the Emma Carlin trail system. [The second road will have a sharp turn followed by a technical climb.]

5.0 mi.   You are at the Emma Carlin trail system. Our suggestion is to ride the outermost section of the green, orange and red trails. There are several great overlook. Especially the Scuppernong Marsh lookout. When returning via the connector trail look for oncoming riders around blind corners.

*The Emma F. Carlin has been under construction in the recent past. Watch for signs indicating the direction of travel on the trail.

Kettle Moraine/Emma F. Carlin

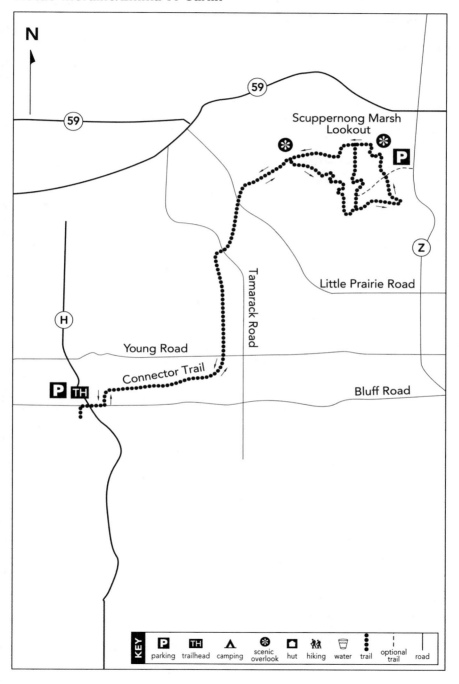

Kettle Moraine/John Muir
Eagle, WI   (414) 594-2135

Distance: 10 miles
Ride time: 1-1.5 hours

Trail: Hard-packed, single-track
Rating: Moderate to Difficult

Access: From Whitewater, WI take Hwy. 12 east to LaGrange. Turn north on Hwy. H at the general store. Drive past first parking area up to Bluff Road. Turn left and park. Public parking is allowed here. Parking sticker is not required but a daily or annual trail pass is. They can be purchased at LaGrange General Store.

0.0 mi.   Across the Bluff Rd. from the parking lot is the short connector trail to the five colored loops of the John Muir trail system.

0.25 mi.   The direction of travel calls for a left turn at this intersection. The suggested 10 mile blue loop immediately greets you with a steep pitch to climb!

1.5 mi.   The first intersection you come to is the crossing of the green and red loops. Follow the red loop and pass the short connector trail to another parking area.

2.0 mi.   This is the intersection of the red and white trail. You want to stay on the outermost sections of each colored loop to ride all of the 10 mile loop. The trail climbs, drops and turns fast and furiously. Many tight off-camber turns test your technical skills.

There will be color-coded marks on posts to alert you to which trail you are on so getting lost is not a concern.

5.0 mi.   At this intersection the white loop meets the blue loop; stay to the left.

8.5 mi.   The blue loop merges with the orange loop.

9.5 mi.   The orange and green trails merge.

10.0 mi.   Look for the connector trail to bring you back to the parking lot.

Kettle Moraine/John Muir

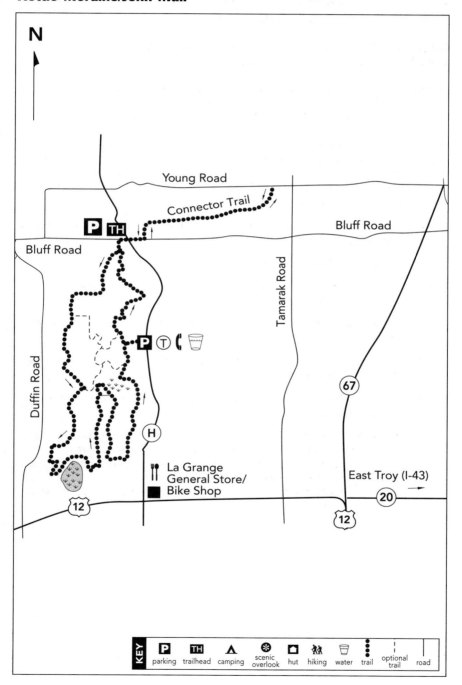

N

Young Road

Connector Trail

P TH

Bluff Road

Bluff Road

Tamarak Road

Duffin Road

P T

67

H

🍴 La Grange
General Store/
■ Bike Shop

East Troy (I-43)

20

12

12

KEY	P	TH	▲	✵	▢	👫	🥛	⋮	┊	
	parking	trailhead	camping	scenic overlook	hut	hiking	water	trail	optional trail	road

Kettle Moraine/Northern Unit
Greenbush, WI   (414) 626-2116

Distance: 13.5 miles
Ride time: 1.5-2 hours

Trail: Hard-packed, ski-trails
Rating: Moderate to Difficult

Access: From Sheboygan, WI take Hwy. 23 west. Go 6 miles west of
Plymouth to Greenbush. Drive south on County Hwy. T for 1.5 miles. Turn left
on Kettle Moraine Drive. Drive 2 miles to picnic/campground area.

*By definition, Kettle Moraine means deep hollows with steep sides that were formed when huge sheets
of ice retreated and ground against each other. What was left behind was a roller coaster terrain
covered with oaks, pines and maples and dotted with marshes. The trail is fast and hard-packed
and will leave you hollering for more. A parking pass and trail pass for riders 16 and older is
required. Toilets, water and picnic area are available.*

0.0 mi.   At the far end of the parking lot by the water pump look for a gravel hill that will
bring you up to the yellow trail. Start the ride to the left.

0.8 mi.   Junction of yellow and pink trails. Stay on the yellow trail.

1.0 mi.   Yellow and green trails merge for a time. We suggest you continue on the
yellow trail for the longest outside loop.

1.8 mi.   You will cross over the horse trail. The riding should be moderate through this
section.

2.1 mi.   The Green trail breaks from the yellow trail. Here the yellow trail winds through
a forest of plantation pine.

3.3 mi.   Stop and take in the view overlooking a vast kettle. The yellow trail gives you
views of Bear Lake and Bear Lake Marsh.

5.4 mi.   Cross over the horse trail again. Soon you will be back at the intersection of
the gravel trail that takes you back to the car. Our suggestions are to finish
the yellow loop then go onto the green trail, the second largest loop and finish
by going on the red and pink trails this gives you more varied terrain. The pink
trail is the most technical, but also the shortest loop. Do them all for a great
afternoon of riding for a total of approximately 14 miles.

Kettle Moraine/Northern Unit

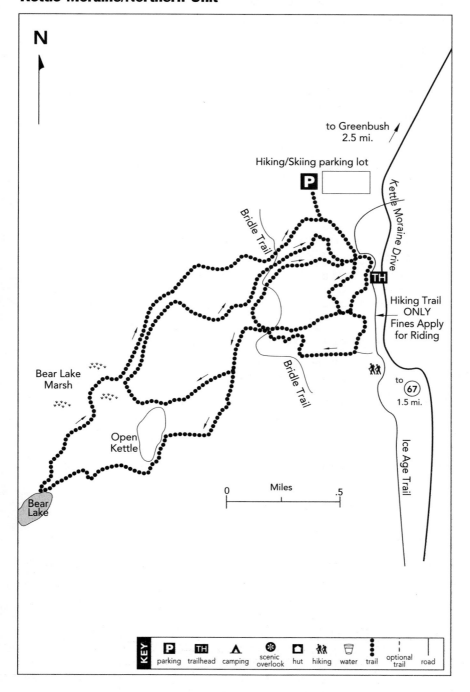

Mirror Lake State Park
Lake Delton, WI   (608) 254-2333

Distance: 8 miles
Ride time: 1-1.5 hours

Trail: Grassy ski trails
Rating: Easy to Moderate

Access: From Madison, WI take I-94 west. Exit at #92 and head south on Highway 12 for 1 mile. Turn west on Fern Dell Road for 1 mile. Park in a lot by the park entrance.

Mirror lake is actually a widening of Dell Creek which meanders quietly towards the Wisconsin River. The mountain bike trails are on the opposite side of the road, but make sure you spend some time "reflecting" on the beautiful water of this large lake.

0.0 mi.   Exit the parking lot and head across the road. The trail starts to the right.

0.1 mi.   The trail hairpins. Turn left at the road. The first 1.5 miles are generally flat as the trail meanders past a small pond and through stands of oak and spruce trees.

0.5 mi.   Come out onto a wide trail. Turn right at the "T". The ski trail winds through stands of red and white pines and then into a forest of hardwoods. Cross the road at 1.5 miles. Take an immediate right and pedal .4 miles around a meadow.

1.9 mi.   Head back into the woods for a fun, fast roll.

2.4 mi.   Cross the road. Pedal a short distance and cross another dirt road near a small inlet to the lake. Follow the tree line.

3.0 mi.   Cross the road into the woods. You ride through an oak savanna upon leaving the woods. Short sections of sand can make the ride tricky. Cross the dirt road at 3.6 miles and pedal through the hardwood forest. Climb a small hill then fly down the other side into a meadow.

4.0 mi.   Cross the road and head to the right up the trail. Ride through the oak and spruce forest.

5.3 mi.   Cross a drainage area and continue forward paralleling the road.

5.5 mi.   Cross road and take the trail to the right. This section becomes a little more hilly.

5.9 mi.   Take the trail to the left and climb the hill (the trail to the right is one way). The terrain requires a little more stamina, but is great riding.

6.6 mi.   The trail comes close to the road but does not cross. Turn left and climb a hill returning into the dense woods. Follow the winding trail back to the road. Cross the road and take the trail to the right. Stay right to go back to the trailhead.

Mirror Lake State Park

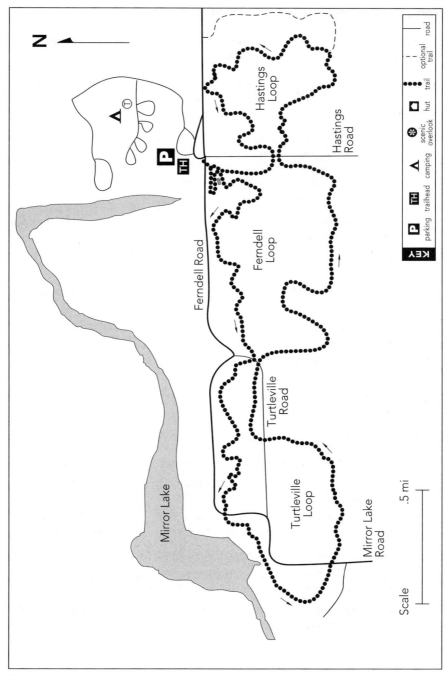

Wisconsin DNR, P.O. Box 7921, Madison, Wisconsin 53707 (608) 266-2181.

Perrot State Park
Trempealeau, WI   (608) 534-6409

Distance: 6 miles   **Trail:** Loop on hard-packed ski trails
Ride time: 1.5 hours   **Rating:** Moderate to Advanced

Access: From Winona, MN cross over the Highway 43 bridge. Take Highway 35 east, 15 miles to Centerville. Turn south on Highway 35 to Trempealeau. Follow state park signs.

Perrot State Park is a diverse mix of marshland, upland fields, steep wooded slopes, cool valleys and dry prairies. The terrain supports hundreds of species of spring wildflowers as well as many species of birds, including some that migrate up the Mississippi River Corridor in the spring and fall. Do not ride this trail system if it is closed. The park people have been known to confiscate bicycles and assess large fines. Call before riding. Water and restrooms are available at the trailhead.

0.0 mi.   Park at the maintenance park office building and gradually climb along the edge of the park through the mixed hardwood forest..

0.4 mi.   Turn left at the first intersection and head onto the Wilbur Trail. Descend the hill into a small meadow.

0.6 mi.   Cross an unmarked foot trail. Pedal through a plantation of beautiful mature white pines.

1.0 mi.   Turn right and head towards Perrot Ridge. There is a section of unmarked trail straight ahead.

1.3 mi.   Ride the black diamond trail for a quarter mile up a moderate incline to a great view on top.

1.5 mi.   Follow the Cedar Glade Trail to the left. (There is a shortcut to the right which avoids the technical sections of this trail.)

2.6 mi.   Climb to the top of Bald Knob for a beautiful view and a much needed rest. This trail is all up or down. The names of the ski trails, "Not So Bad Run," "Ski Jump Hill" and "Valley Run" give you an idea of the steep descents.

3.5 mi.   Climb another hill until you switch back to the left. Welcome to the "not so flat Midwest."

3.6 mi.   Stay right at this intersection. The trail soon "Y's". Stay left for the suggested ride or turn right and hike to the top of Perrot ridge for another great overlook.

4.2 mi.   The bike trail heads right for a nice view of the Mississippi River Valley.

4.7 mi.   Turn left onto the grassy trail and curve back to the right over a hill. The downhill has erosion control timbers across the trail so be careful.

5.0 mi.   Pedal straight down the hill to a four-way intersection. Take the trail to the left back to the trailhead.

Perrot State Park

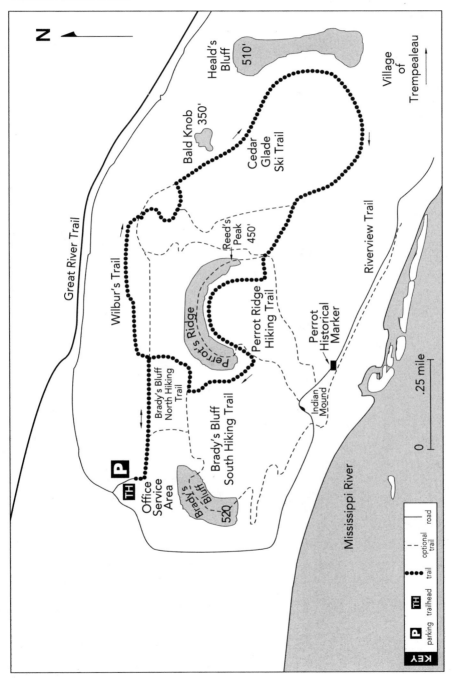

Wisconsin DNR, P.O. Box 7921, Madison, Wisconsin 53707 (608) 266-2181.

Smrekar Trail
Millston, WI   (715) 284-1426

Distance: 7.5 miles
Ride Time: 1.5-2 hours

Trail: Grass/dirt ski trail, some sand
Rating: Moderate to Advanced

Access: Black River State Forest is located 12 miles SE of Black River Falls on I-94. Exit at Millston. Go northeast on County Highway O to Rustic Road Turn left on Rustic Road to North Settlement Road. Take a right and drive 2.5 miles. Park in the Wildcat parking lot. There are outhouses and water available at the trailhead.

The state forest lies along the margin of the glaciated central plain, and the "driftless" area of Wisconsin. Unglaciated buttes, sandstone hills, and limestone bluffs, such as Castle Mound, dot the vast forest landscape. The Winnebago have used this land as a meeting ground for centuries. (This area was the scene of many conflicts as invading tribes met in battle.)

0.0 mi.   From the Wildcat parking lot, ride east across North Settlement Road and follow a link trail to the North Trail intersection.

0.2 mi.   Turn right and wind through red pines. Look to your right for a great view of buttes jutting into the sky. There are several moderate climbs in this section.

1.5 mi.   Pedal onto the Central Trail. Just after the intersection there is an old cemetery to your right.

2.1 mi.   Ride through the intersection that joins the West Loop.

3.0 mi.   Stay right where the trail splits. Veer left on the East Loop link trail to the next intersection and follow the signs leading you to an old farmstead with root cellar, old foundation, and well. Double back to the intersection of the East and West Loop. Ride through the parking lot onto the South Loop. Ignore the "do not enter" sign. This section is a rolling trail through woodlands.

4.1 mi.   Turn right at this "Y" intersection, and ride a short distance on the East Loop.

4.3 mi.   Veer right on the Ridge Trail. Be prepared for a strenuous, technical climb that takes you up to the top of the ridge for great, panoramic views. This wooded ridge gives you many opportunities to stop, take a break, and snap a couple of pictures.

4.9 mi.   EXPERTS ONLY!! Take a right onto a seldom used section of the Ridge Trail that has steep pitches.

5.3 mi.   Turn right. (The shortcut joins from the left.) Cruise along the top of this beautiful ridge. Continue through the next intersection.

6.4 mi.   The Ridge Trail intersects with the North Loop. Cross the North Trail Loop. Here the trail is flatter and passes through stands of plantation pines.

7.4 mi.   Turn right and backtrack on the link trail. Cross over Smrekar Road to the Wildcat parking lot.

Smrekar Trail-Black River State Forest

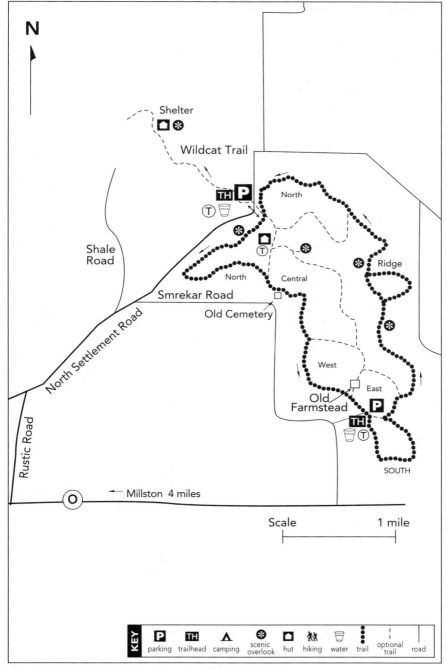

N

Shelter

Wildcat Trail

TH P
T

North

Shale
Road

North

Central

Ridge

Smrekar Road

Old Cemetery

West

East

Old
Farmstead

P
TH
T

SOUTH

North Settlement Road

Rustic Road

Millston 4 miles

Scale   1 mile

KEY | P parking | TH trailhead | ▲ camping | ✷ scenic overlook | ☐ hut | 🚶 hiking | water | trail | optional trail | road

Wisconsin DNR, P.O. Box 7921, Madison, Wisconsin 53707 (608) 266-2181.

Wildcat Trail
Millston, WI   (715) 284-1426

Distance: 7.1 miles   **Trail:** Loop, grass/dirt ski trail, some sand
Ride time: 1-1.5 hours   **Rating:** Moderate to Advanced

Access: Black River State Forest is located 12 miles SE of Black River Falls on I-94. Exit at Millston. Go northeast on County Highway O to Rustic Road. Turn left on Rustic Road to North Settlement Road. Take a right and go 2.5 miles. Park in the Wildcat parking lot.

The Black River State Forest boasts 24 miles of awesome mountain biking. The horizon is shaped by the limestone bluffs that rise above the forest. Indian tribes often met in battle on nearby grounds. Water and outhouses are available at the trailhead. A wheel trail pass is required to ride in the Black River State Forest.

0.0 mi.   The Red Oak loop is on the northwest side of the parking lot. Follow this trail in the opposite direction of the ski traffic. Enjoy riding through the dense forest of mixed hardwoods.

1.5 mi.   Veer right and continue through the next intersection. Go around the gate and cross Shale Road. Ride around the second gate.

1.7 mi.   Go left at this two-way intersection. Climb to a scenic point for spectacular views of buttes and sandstone hills jutting into the sky. You are now on the Wildcat Ski loop.

2.0 mi.   Ride through this intersection.

2.4 mi.   (The trail on your right is a short cut to the east side of Wildcat loop.)

2.7 mi.   You can visit a scenic overview by taking this trail on the right.

4.9 mi.   The shortcut trail joins from the right. Ride through the thick forest on rolling terrain.

5.4 mi.   The Wildcat trailhead intersects here. Cross Shale Road. Turn right onto the Norway Pine loop and ride against the ski traffic signs. This section of the Norway Pine loop is very challenging with some steep climbs. Your reward is great vistas with benches perfect for catching your breath.

7.1 mi.   Return to parking lot.

A trail map is available for rides not listed in this book.

Wildcat Trail-Black River State Forest

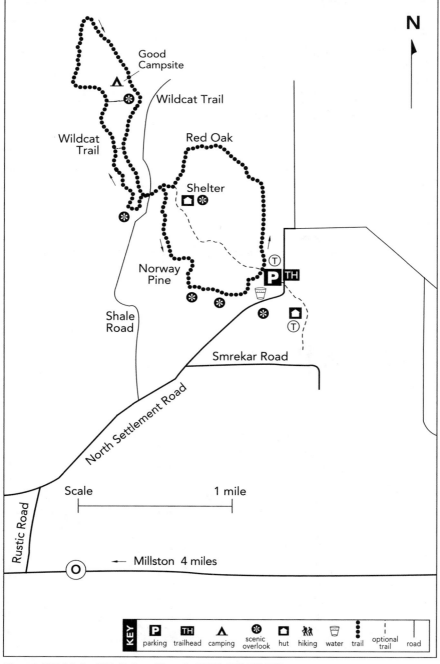

Wisconsin DNR, P.O. Box 7921, Madison, Wisconsin 53707 (608) 266-2181.

PLAN AHEAD!

IMBA Rules of the Trail

Minnesota State Trails

Cannon Valley Trail:
19.7 miles, from Red Wing to Cannon Falls, MN.
A paved trail that parallels the south side of the Cannon River.
A daily wheel pass is required.
Red Wing Trailhead: From Highway 61, exit on Wither's Harbor drive.
Turn on Old West Main Street for one block.
Cannon Falls Trailhead: Off of Hwy. 19 one block west of stoplight.
(612) 296-6157

Douglas State Trail:
13 miles one-way from Rochester to Pine Island, MN.
The trail surface is paved. The Douglas trail crosses the Plum Creek
and Zumbro River.
Rochester Trailhead: Hwy. 52 take the IBM exit and head west to
County Road 4. Pine Island Trailhead: Pine Island City Park on County
Road 11.
(612) 296-6157

Heartland State Trail:
28 miles from Park Rapids to Cass Lake, MN.
The trail is paved. This area is home to the largest bald eagle
population in the lower 48 states.
Park Rapids Trailhead: Heartland County Park at 5th Street. West of
Co. Rd. 99.
Walker Trailhead: .5 miles south of Highway 371.
(612) 296-6157

Luce Line State Trail:
30 miles, from Plymouth to Winsted, MN. Crushed limestone.
Vicksburg Lane Trailhead: Between County Road 6 and 15.
Winsted Lake Trailhead: South of County Road 6.
(612) 540-0234

Paul Bunyan State Trail:
The Paul Bunyan State Trail; 100 miles from Brainerd, MN to Lake
Bemidji State Park. This is considered the longest contiguous "rails to
trails" conversion in the world. This new trail is in the final stages of
completion. There will be four river crossings and many trailheads.
(218) 829-2838

Root River State Trail:
28.5 paved miles with 48 bridge crossings, from Fountain to Rushford, MN. Take a ride along the scenic river bluffs and through historic towns.
Fountain Trailhead: County Road 8; go one mile east of Fountain.
Rushford Trailhead: Elm Street next to depot.
(507) 886-2230

Sakatah Singing Hills State Trail:
39 mile trail parallels the Cannon River from Mankato to Faribault in the transition zone of the "Big Woods" and prairies.
The trail is crushed limestone.
Mankato trailhead: Lime Valley Road northwest of town.
Sakatah Lake State Park Trailhead: 2 miles east of Waterville.

Willard Munger/Carlton-Duluth Segment State Trail:
14.5 miles, from Carlton to the southwest end of Duluth, MN.
The trail surface is paved. Cross the cascading water of the St. Lawrence River on an old railroad bridge.
Carlton Trailhead: Highway 210 to County Road 1 south.
West Duluth Trailhead: Off of Highway 23 on 75th Ave.

Willard Munger/Hinckley Fire Segment State Trail:
37 miles, from Hinckley to Barnum, MN. The trail is paved.
This tree-lined route passes through farmlands and meadows.
Hinckley Trailhead: County Road 18 west of Highway 61.
Moose Lake Trailhead: Highway 61 at the Moose River.

Gateway Trail:
16.9 mile trail, 9.7 miles dual trail. The trail surface is paved.
This segment of the Willard Munger Trail will take you through urban areas, wooded countryside and fields.
West: Three miles north of St. Paul on 35E, exit at Larpenteur.
East: Pine Park Point. North of Stillwater 5 miles on Co. Rd. 55.

Taconite State Trail:
165 miles, from Grand Rapids to Ely. Natural surface.
This rustic stretch of trail meanders through countryside thick with lakes, hardwood forests and access to four state parks.
McCarthy Beach State Park: 17 miles north of Chisholm on Highway 73.
Trailheads can also be found in Grand Rapids and Ely.

Minnesota Department of Natural Resources:
Phone (612) 296-6157   (From MN) 800-766-6000

Wisconsin State Trails

Cheese Country Recreation Trail:
47 miles. Trail surface is crushed limestone. Former railroad corridor located in the heart of a three-county area boasting over 30 cheese factories.
Phone (608)325-7648

Elroy-Sparta State Trail:
33 miles. Crushed limestone surface. The "Granddaddy" of them all. A delightful 33-mile roll through wooded valleys and friendly small towns. There are three century-old tunnels on the trail.
Phone (608)337-4775

400 Bike Trail:
20 miles. Crushed limestone surface. The somewhat hilly terrain features rock outcroppings along the Baraboo River.
Phone (608)254-2333

Great River State Trail:
22.5 miles. This trail follows the shore of the mighty Mississippi.
Phone (608)534-6409

Lacrosse River State Trail:
21.5 miles. Crushed limestone. Developed from an abandoned rail line, this 21.5-mile trail is a delightful ride along the LaCrosse River.
Phone (608)782-2366

Military Ridge State Trail:
39.5 mile, graded and surface of packed limestone. High point on the trail is at Blue Mounds, almost 1300 feet above sea level. The lowest point on the trail is along the Sugar River between Riley and Verona, about 930 feet.
Phone (608) 935-2315

Red Cedar State Trail:
This 14-mile trail parallels the river from Menomonie through the historic lumber town of Downsville, to the great Chippewa River Valley.
Phone (715) 232-2631

Sugar River State Trail:

23 miles, surface is packed limestone. Level route crosses over streams rushing on trestle bridges carrying you through picturesque scenes of rolling hills, meadows and state wildlife refuges.
Phone (608) 527-2334

Tuscobia-Park Falls State Trail:

76 miles, from Tuscobia to Park Falls. This is a rough trail and has not been resurfaced with many undeveloped sections which may have rough or soft areas.

Tuscobia-Park Falls State Trail

Department of Natural Resources
Rt. 2, Box 2003, Hayward, WI 54843

Chippewa River Trail:

23 miles from Eau Claire to junction with the Red Cedar River State Trail. State trail pass required.
1-800-344-FUNN

RiDe ON OPeN tRAiLS ONLY!

IMBA Rules of the Trail

Contact Organizations

Minnesota

Minnesota Mountain Bike
Resource Group
15251 Greenhave Drive, #111
Burnsville, MN 55306
(612) 452-9736

Minnesota DNR
500 Lafayette Road, Box 40
St. Paul, MN 55155
(800) 766-6000
(612) 296-6157

Minnesota Travel
Information Center
375 Jackson St.,
250 Skyway Level
St. Paul, MN 55101
(800) 657-3700
(612) 296-5029

Superior National Forest
P.O. Box 338
Duluth, MN 55801
(218) 720-5324

Chippewa National Forest
Cass Lake, MN 56633
(218) 335-8600

Wisconsin

CAMBA
Chequamegon Area
Mountain Bike Association
P.O. Box 141
Cable, WI 54821
(800) 533-7454

Wisconsin DNR
P.O. Box 7921
Madison, WI 53707
(608) 266-2181
(608) 266-2621

USDA Forest Service
310 West Wisconsin Avenue,
Room 500
Milwaukee, WI 53203
(608) 266-0842

Chequamegon National Forest
USDA-Forest Service
1170 South 4th Avenue
Park Falls, WI 54552
(715) 762-2461

Wisconsin Division of Tourism
Box 7606
Madison, WI 53707
(800) 372-2737
(608) 266-2161

National Bike Organizations

IMBA
International Mountain Bicycling
Association
P.O. Box 412043
Los Angeles, CA 90041
(818) 792-8830

NORBA
1 Olympic Plaza
Colorado Springs, CO 80909
(719) 578-4717

WCC
Women's Cycling Coalition
P.O. Box 281
Louisville, CO 80027
(303) 666-0500

Leave No tRAce!

IMBA Rules of the Trail

Who are these people?

Cindy Storm

Cindy has won the Chequamegon Fat-Tire "Short and Fat" (or Short and Smart, as she says) for the last five years. In addition she has won numerous other titles throughout Minnesota and Wisconsin. She is a natural mechanic and could win awards for her ability to "wrench" on the trail. Her love for outdoor activities takes Cindy to her cabin in the Chequamegon National Forest area with its abundant trail system. "Storm" also bakes a great cookie!

Cindy Bijold

Bikes are "B"'s life, that's why we call her "the gidget head." Cindy has an obsession with weight, not her own—her bike's! She has worked with the Hennepin County Park Board: (Minneapolis, MN) to open access to mountain biking in the Hennepin county Parks. In addition she has been involved with MMBRG, (Metro Mountain Biking Resource Group), an organization dedicated to promoting the sport of mountain biking. Cindy is a tough, regional racer finishing in the top five, several times, in the Chequamegon "Fat-Tire 40". The original idea for this book came out of her head and is a wizard at marketing.

Who are these people?

Kelley Owen

Kelley "thinks" she is an average competitor. An All-American, a member of the USA National Women's Hockey Team and a second place finish, behind Cindy Storm, in the "1993 Chequamegon Short and Fat.c" Is that average? Kelley says she usually places better when the "Cindy's" are not in her age bracket. She is always up for an adventure and lets herself get talked into anything her friends can think of, including this book! It was an adventure and a learning experience to be remembered.

Anne Breckenridge

Anne is a self-proclaimed amateur athlete and professional participant. She will do a race if you can guarantee it will be fun. Anne pushed us to believe that we could actually write this book. In her persistance Anne made us ride trails in places like the Sand Dune State Forest. (Wasn't the name a clue?) And the Finland State Forest where we portaged our bikes for 1/2 a mile before she would let us quit. (That trail didn't make the book either.) Her determination to find good, interesting trails allowed us to find areas that we never would have dreamed existed.

Order Form

"Using THE NORTH COUNTRY GUIDE TO MOUNTAIN BIKING, planning rides to accommodate personal skill level and riding fitness are easy to do. For anyone planning a trip into the north country, this book is a must.

Cindy Whitehead
National Downhill, Slalom,
Cross-Country Champion
1986-1993

To Order Additional Copies of:

The Northcountry Guide To
Mountain Biking
Minnesota • Wisconsin

Send check or money order to:
White Pines Press, Inc.
5311 South Park Circle, Suite 300
Savage, MN 55378
Phone: (612) 440-6394   Fax: (612) 890-8701

Please Send _____ copies @ $14.95 Each _____

MN residents add 6.5% sales tax   _____

Shipping and Handling   + $3.00

TOTAL: $_____

PLEASE SHIP TO: _____

ADDRESS: _____

CITY: _____ STATE _____ ZIP _____